For Dr. Irwing R[...]
my thanks for his wonderful
hospitality.

Cordially,

Julian Ardila

WALDEN THREE

WALDEN THREE
A Scientific Utopia

by

Ruben Ardila, Ph.D.

A Geneva Book

Carlton Press, Inc. New York, NY

© 1990 by Ruben Ardila
ALL RIGHTS RESERVED
Manufactured in the United States of America
ISBN 0-8062-3309-5

TABLE OF CONTENTS

Harvard	11
Martin Luther King	15
Revolution	20
The New Government	25
The Children First	30
The Calendar Reform	37
China or the USSR?	47
Social Communication	54
Education	60
Family and Sexuality	65
The Old People	70
Maribel	74
The Army and the Police	79
The New Family Structure	83
School and Society	89
Can Science Save Us?	95
The Place of Religion	99
Neither Marx nor Jesus	104
The Experimental Analysis	107
The Experimental Synthesis	112
Mercedes and Felipe	117
Delinquency and Criminality	122
Ecology	130
Freedom and Determinism	134
The End	139

With only one life
I will not learn enough;
with the light of other lives
other lives will live in my songs.
   Pablo Neruda

Do you say that nothing is created?
It does not matter. With the mud
of the earth, make a cup
for your brother to drink.
   Antonio Machado

There is only a man on earth
and his name is All Men.
There is only one woman on earth
and her name is All Women.
There is only one child on earth
and the child's name is All the Children of the World.
   The Family of Man

WALDEN THREE

CHAPTER 1
HARVARD

Sad faces, happy faces, smiling faces, serious faces, faces that pass by, faces that look and leave, faces that will stay with me forever although they may not know it, beautiful faces, ugly faces, old faces, young faces, faces, faces. . . .

While the plane flew over the Canal, I thought about all these faces. I thought about my four years at Harvard, that so important period of my life that had gone and would never return. I thought about the world that awaited me in Panama and the world I had left behind at Harvard. Four years. . . . It seemed unbelievable: one day my adviser told me that my Ph.D. dissertation had been approved and that we should set a date for the oral examination which would take place within a few weeks. The next thing I remember was a long parade of people dressed in caps and gowns, all very artificial, all very false, all very Harvard.

What upset me most about leaving Harvard was having to give up my little room that looked out over a meadow, where I had spent my days and nights trying to find out everything that had been written about experimental psychology, which I supposedly should know about before getting my doctorate. A Ph.D. in Psychology from Harvard. Fantastic. And now, what was I going to do in South America with my doctorate? One alternative was to stay in the United States, not at Harvard, but at Alabama or South Dakota or at some other university where they would need me. There was always the possibility of becoming a professor, of discovering why laboratory rats follow Skinner's principles and not Hull's, of writing for the APA (American Psychological Association) journals and of presenting papers at the annual meetings of such a scholarly organization.

I did not want to leave my room at Harvard. The United States could go to hell, as it was bound to sooner or later, it made no difference to me. But Harvard, in Cambridge, Massachusetts, which is close to the river and close to Boston, was a "wonderland," a kind of oasis. Even if the United States did collapse, my room would be there forever: the room where I had studied for four years, where I had drunk beer with my friends, and where I tried to go to bed with Karen, a girl with blue eyes and a silly smile, who had looked at me in horror when I had kissed her and fondled her breasts, and had freed herself, run down the steps and escaped never to return.

My room had been the frame of reference of my life. My books, my music, my paintings, a photograph of my parents taken in South America many years ago before I came to Harvard, were all there. One day, like any other, I was sitting in my room staring into space when Pierre, a French boy who lived next door and who was also studying for his doctorate in psychology, came in to give me a copy of a journal of psychology.

"David, look, in Panama they need a professor of psychology for the Central University. Aren't you from Panama? I am sorry. I know you're not . . . But why don't you apply for this job anyhow? It's cut out for you; I would go if I could speak Spanish. However as you know it was quite a task for me to learn English, and it would be even more difficult to learn Spanish. But you, old man, you're just the man for this job."

"Panama?"

"Yes, Panama, the gateway to South America where the Canal is. I think, old man, you would feel at home there. It's a contract for two years, they give round-trip transportation for you and your family, compensation for the tropical climate . . . I really don't know what that means. They should give us compensation for coming to these freezing countries, but for going to Panama . . . *Mon Dieu,* it's a crazy world!"

"Panama, Panama. . . ."

"The place where Americans have done and undone, where they built a zone for themselves, with fields, schools, television, and signs in English, and above all electric fences so that the Panamanian people cannot enter and soil such beauty. Panama, where the national currency is on a par with the dollar, where there are more illiterates than in the rest of Latin America, where you can get latest model American cars while half the population walk around barefoot. A great country, for a man like you, old man, since you're so interested in sociology. Have I ever told you that you should be a sociologist and not an experimental psychologist? Anyway, social problems interest you, although you're a quiet man who appears to be indifferent.... Deep down you become incensed when you see such things happen.... Old man, I remember when you told me your impressions of Washington the day they killed Dr. King, and you saw how the Negroes set fire to the Capital of the United States. The city was burning from top to bottom: buildings, trees, people, even the lakes and the monuments, everything was consumed, and a red blood-like stain formed on the horizon. I remember that you said it was the dust reflecting the color of the fire, but I'm sure, old man, that you thought it was blood, the blood of Dr. King, the blood of the blacks assassinated by the whites and of the whites assassinated by the blacks. You became incensed, and I said to myself, gee, Dave is interested in all this shit, the blacks asking for a better life and the whites doing their best not to give it to them.... Anyway, my friend, you worry so much about the tremendous chaos in this twentieth century world, and I feel you ought to give way to your natural impulses and satisfy your interest in society. This is why I suggest you go to Panama. There, the blacks don't ask for justice; nor do the whites kill the blacks. But the 'gringos' are sucking the blood of the Panamanians and the day will come when the whole situation will explode.... Doesn't it sound like fun?"

"Fun! And why don't you go?"

"I already told you, boy, it's because of the language. When my adviser gave me the results of the Differential Aptitude Test, he told me that I was good at many things, among others, mathematics, psychology, physics, all the sciences, but that language wasn't my strong point. *C'est la vie!* ... Otherwise, I would go to the Third World. It's an arsenal; it's a laboratory, much better than the costly ones we have here at Harvard in William James Hall."

"I'll think about it, Pierre. I really don't know what to do. I've been buried under books for four years and I haven't a clue what's going on in the outside world."

"Yes, my friend, coming to Harvard meant something like being shut up in an ivory tower without a window, it meant to study morning, noon and night, including Saturdays and Sundays. For me, coming to America was a marvelous idea ... pardon me, to North America, I know you South Americans, are also Americans and you feel very offended when the 'gringos'—to hell with them—apply the term 'American' for themselves only. . . . Anyway, in France, when I received the letter of acceptance from Harvard, I felt as if I could touch the sky. Here, I have met a couple of good professors, a lot of mediocre, snob, pedantic, simple and good people, all kinds. I have met foreigners like you, the son of the ex-shah of Persia, the nephew of the ex-king of Greece and other such specimens. Harvard has been a great experience."

"I found Harvard a friendly place and not too difficult."

"Sure. What's difficult is getting in. After that the ball rolls, you take exams, write what the professors want you to write, lie, contradict yourself, carry out a couple of investigations, projects that don't contribute anything to the advance of science, but are methodologically perfect, even though the results are practically meaningless. And one fine day you receive your Master's degree and, almost without knowing it, a few years later, your doctorate. Ph.D. in Psychology. God, it sounds really great! I'm not going back to France, I'm thinking of staying in America, I'll change my name to Peter, get married to an American girl and have a couple of 'gringo' children. France cheated me, my dear friend."

"I don't know what to do, but I would like to go back to Latin America, to the Third World."

"You have a whole world to build there. Europe, on the other hand, is dead and buried, it's a museum and one can't live in a museum. The future is on this side of the Atlantic, in Cuba, in Colombia, in Brazil which is so large and green, in Canada . . . even here in this hell hole, the United States. I'm not going back to France. I remember my mother and my brothers drinking wine every day at breakfast and spending half the day drunk. I remember my father, years ago, in a cafe arguing in favor of the government while pounding on the wooden table. We're peasants you know. I came to America on a scholarship just like you; we're a couple of poor devils in the the richest country in the world. My father is still poor, and my brothers are peasants in France who work from dawn to dusk. I'd like to see them again, you know. I remember my mother's sad eyes as she said good-bye at the airport, when the plane that would take me from Paris to Boston was about to take off. That seems almost an eternity ago. Now I belong to this part of the world. Maybe I'll go to French Canada or I'll just stay in America."

"In North America, you mean."

"Of course."

"Panama. I've never thought of that country as a place to work. I don't know if I should think about it more. It seems a good idea, Pierre . . ."

A few weeks later, I said good-bye to all my schoolmates and left the United States, destination Panama. It was a polite and simple parting since the Anglo-Saxon culture does not go in for expressing profound emotions. Besides, it was logical that I should leave. I had already finished my doctorate, and there was no reason why I should stay in Cambridge devoting my time exclusively to conjuring up memories, walking through the laboratories in William James Hall and thinking of all the happy experiences I had had at Harvard.

The plane circled Panama City and I stretched my neck to see as much as I could. There was my new home for the next few years. A relatively big tropical city, the capital of a Central American Country, important all over the world for its Canal. Panama, Panama, what would be waiting for me there? I was happy and sad at the same time. I thought about my room at Harvard, about my friends, about the sad faces, happy faces, smiling faces, worried faces, faces that I had left behind and the many faces I would find in my new world. The Third World.

CHAPTER 2
MARTIN LUTHER KING

The main room was full of smoke, and hardly anything could be seen. Voices could be heard which were speaking English and Spanish with a strong English accent. There were songs and laughter. I had arrived late for the party because I had not been too interested in going but had changed my mind at the last minute. The North American professors from the Central University were giving a party, and counted on my presence since I had just arrived from the United States. I did not know anyone in the city and they wanted to be kind to me. The room was full of people and not only university professors. It was late after twelve midnight, and, as I soon realized, everyone was quite drunk. Some people were hugging each other, many were singing, others burst into laughter.

"David González! Welcome. It's wonderful to have you with us. Come on, man, I want you to meet Mr. Duffy, Dr. Swanson, and Mrs. Campbell. Make yourself at home, Dave, we're so glad you could come even though you got here late."

"Please excuse all the confusion, David. May I call you by your first name?"

"Of course, Mrs. Campbell."

"You know how the Americans are. They take advantage of any party like this to get drunk and have fun until they collapse. Tonight, Friday, or really Saturday early morning because it's quite late, by the way, is the day of "id," everyone giving way to their bad instincts. That's the way the Americans are. I came to Panama with my husband—I don't know where he is, he must be in the next room—many years ago. We thought of staying only a year, at the most two. Now I've lost count."

"Don't you like it here?"

"No. This is a country of negroes. Everything is disorganized, I hate the heat, the people, the political problems. I want to go back to Wisconsin, there is nothing like Wisconsin. Have you ever been in Milwaukee?"

"No, never."

"I understand you're new here, that you've just arrived from the States and you're trying to educate the asses that attend this university. You should have stayed in the States. There, everything is so clean, functional and orderly. I'm going to return one of these days."

In the other room there was a group singing songs about the Spanish Civil War, some in English and others in Spanish with a terrible accent. I looked around at the rest of the guests, and I could not see one Panamanian. The predominant language was English and almost everyone looked North American. I felt a bit uncomfortable, mainly because I only knew two or three people, but also because there was no one from my culture. A group of drunks could be heard singing:

"If there's a God in heaven, let the tables turn!
If there's a God in heaven, let the tables turn!
Let the poor eat bread, let the poor eat bread
and the rich, shit, shit!

> Let the poor eat bread, let the poor eat bread
> and the rich, shit, shit!"

Everything was such a mess that soon it seemed quite comical. I served myself a double whiskey with soda from the house bar and kept on walking by the various groups. One of the professors was telling a story in English about one of his especially dumb students, and I got closer to listen.

"So I thought the best thing for poor Perez was to read a book by Gamow, since he had been unable to understand the basic principles of modern physics. I think it's too difficult for the Latin American brain. Ha, ha, ha! So I gave him a book by Gamow, I don't remember which one, it was a Spanish translation of course. In it was an historical description of the difficulties the scientist went through to discover the principle of increasing entropy. And there was a half-joking short poem in the book:

> 'Decrease, increase,
> Increase, decrease,
> What do I care what entrophy does.'

Well, this ass Perez read the book. He liked it a lot and a few days later he commented that what he liked best was the poem which went like this:

> 'Increase, decrease, decrease, increase,
> What do I care what electrotherapy does.'

Everyone laughed heartily and so did I. It seemed to me impossible to confuse entropy with electrotherapy, but that is the way things go.

"Every nation has what it deserves," said a voice in the corner, in the best midwest English. "Us, Americans, we deserve Nixon, Johnson, Carter and other such idiots. And these Latins deserve their dictators their military, their Perons...."

"I have the solution for Panama: convert it into the fifty first state of the United States of America, or the fifty second after Puerto Rico. That way they will be Americans and could feel proud that we are here, with the Canal and everything else."

"There's just one problem, man: the race would deteriorate. There are too many colored people here, almost everyone. We have enough trouble with Alabama, Chicago, the blacks who stir up trouble and attempt to burn America from North to South, from the Canadian to the Mexican border ... poor America.

Burned by her ungrateful adopted children who came from Africa to work on the cotton plantations in the South. . . ."

"What beasts, what beasts . . ."

"If the tables were turned, we would eat shit and they would live in the Canal zone with clean schools, paved streets, palm trees, supermarkets, abundance, dollars, Cadillacs . . . while we would live in the dirty streets of Panama or Colon; barefoot, sunburned, looking for work, with a pregnant wife, a sick child and no money to pay the rent."

"I remember an article about Thanksgiving in an American newspaper that made fun of underdeveloped countries. It said that the Latin Americans should pray on Thanksgiving: "Thank thee, Oh Lord, for my sick wife, for my drunken father, for my brother who died from a curable disease, for my rachitic son, for my mother who prays all day long instead of working, for the children sleeping in the streets, for the rats that run about the house and for the cockroaches that share my ration of rice. . . . Thank thee, Oh Lord."

"Some Panamanians became communists. Everyone knows that story. Their first step was to burn the American flag and stone the houses of the rich. Because the rich are on our side, you know. Those sons of bitches are students besides being communists and they're getting organized for guerrilla warfare. They want to go to China for training and then come back and throw us, Americans, out of Panama territory once and for all. But they're such blockheads that they're apt to just talk and not do anything. The Panamanians talk and talk and talk. Finally they grow up, they get a job in an American company and their revolutionary spirit dies a sudden death. They're forever teenagers, poor things."

"I feel sorry for them, Swanson. I don't think they're so bad."

"Sorry? Life's a struggle, the survival of the fittest. I am drunk, I know. And I'm furious, and I hate the Panamanians and I hate my work and I hate this Negro country. I want to go back to America where people are civilized. But even though I'm drunk, I'm honest enough to recognize that they're powerful and we should be afraid of them. The leader of the left-wing party is a 21-year-old boy called Martin Luther King. What a coincidence, no? He's a Negro, blacker than the devil's arse. I think besides being a student he's a military man. And he's black. Black as the conscience of the communists. And very dangerous."

"Martin Luther King . . . "

"I think it's a pseudonym, but whether it's his name or not, I hope that some day someone gets the good idea of wiping him off the map."

Many people were listening to this man of undefinable age and blood-shot eyes. Many others kept on drinking and singing. I do not know how, but all of a sudden, I found myself in the middle of a group of young people in another room. I think it was near dawn and we had all drunk too much. In this enormous house, at this hour and with so many guests, I do not know how there had been enough whiskey for everyone. I was hungry, hot, tieless and suffocating. My interlocutor was a young man who appeared to be about 25, like me, and looked like a Negro athlete, a kind of boxing champion. But he had a slender body, intelligent-looking eyes and a nice manly smile.

"Psychologist from Harvard?" he was asking me. "Maybe you're the man I need to change the world. You know Skinner, right? I've read a lot about him, his books, his ideas, those strange ideas he has about freedom and dignity. I think Skinner has real power which he's never used. He's a scientist, the only man who knows how to handle human beings. I have great respect for scientific psychology. Many times during the lectures on psychology that I attended when I was a political science student in the United States, I argued in favor of Skinner. I don't think that anyone has really understood him, that with his ideas it's possible to change the world."

I looked at him without saying anything. He spoke passionately, with a kind of religious fervor. My relationship with Skinner had been very sporadic and this demi-god of behaviorism was now really more of a philosopher than a laboratory investigator, and at Harvard almost no one took him very seriously. They respected him, all right, but though that he was past it.

"Psychology is the most important of all the sciences, it's the science of the future," went on my interlocutor. "I would have studied psychology, but I think the problems of political science are more urgent and important, and decisive, and terrible than the problems of psychology. Let's be friends, professor. I'm going to become involved in politics and I'll make this planet shake. I'm going to change the world, change the course of history. They'll talk about me the length and breadth of this planet, just as they talk about Castro, Lenin, Khomeini and even Christ. I want, you know . . . I . . . "

"And what role do you want psychology to play?"

"Psychology? Or rather you. The role. . . . What role? Yes, I'm sorry, it's this damn whiskey. I think operant psychology has the principles and the laws to change the world, but it doesn't have the power. I, on the contrary, think I'm going to have the power very soon. I want you to join me. I want you with your scientific knowledge to help me change the world, and create a perfect society, a utopia, a *Walden Two* which will surpass the dreams of Skinner, Plato, Sir Thomas More. I have all the defects in the world: I'm frustrated, I'm a potential killer, I'm . . . no, I'd rather not say it yet. But I also have some qualities, professor, I have something you don't, balls, and you have something I don't, science, knowledge. . . ."

"Where did you study?"

"In the school of life, brother. I pulled myself out of the gutter, I travelled, I studied, I got degrees, I quickly worked my way up. I have a high rank in the Army. Even though, I'm black, I've come a long way. And I'm young, brother, just like you. How old are you?"

"I'm about to turn 27."

"You look younger than that, really. I want you to be my friend anyway. Your name is David, right? Doctor David González, Ph.D. in Behavioral Psychology, from Harvard, obtained under Skinner. Together we can make the biggest scientific and social experiment in history. I'm Negro but I'm strong, intelligent, I want to go far, I want. . . . Give me another drink David, all of a sudden I feel sick . . . you know, it's late. . . ."

"What's your name?"

"Martin Luther King."

CHAPTER 3
REVOLUTION

Time went by and I renewed my university activities. I continued reading and studying. I tried to organize a laboratory for experimental psychology, with pigeons, rats and automatic recording, but I did not succeed. The dean felt that the students would be against it because it was "Imperialist" and "fascist." The students were not at all interested in the laboratory, but I think I succeeded in making a name for myself as a good professor. I worried a lot about my students. It was necessary to struggle and struggle; to learn and to teach elementary things which I thought people already knew.

The books did not arrive. No one received journals. There were no congresses or scientific psychologists in the country. People travelled a lot, but not for academic purposes, and without a doubt no one thought that science could be done here. I did not lose hope, but my efforts were almost in vain.

Slowly I was losing the notion of psychology as a laboratory science. I was losing the context of my discipline, of my university, of everything that before had been so important. It was like being dragged along by a river without knowing where it was going, but sure it was not taking the right course. I felt lost, as if I were floating in space in a strange world. Anyway it was the Third World. And I had chosen it, conscious of its limitations and also of its possibilities.

Years went by. My parents came to see me a couple of times. Then my mother died and my father went to live with my sister and her husband. I saw less and less of my family although I wanted to keep in touch with them. I travelled less, I went to fewer congresses, I read fewer scientific journals. I was becoming more and more out of touch with the past and growing as mediocre as my companions at the university who were only interested in their salary and how to avoid student problems.

The country had a democratic government, but things were going very badly. There were a lot of social and economic problems, and unemployment was high. The military threatened to take power and to establish a right-wing dictatorship. The students hated the government and hated the military and said the only solution was a system such as Cuba had. The professors were afraid of the government and the military, but especially afraid of the students.

I was very alone. It was strange. I did not keep in touch with my sister, my aging father or with my schoolmates from Harvard. I travelled very little and felt my life was empty and meaningless. It was partly due to my shyness, to my introversion and to my incapability to make new friends.

I thought of getting married because it might solve my existential problems. There were a few fat and silly girls in love with me to whom it would have been very easy to propose. There was one I felt very attracted to, who was neither fat nor silly and who stirred my naughtiest thoughts, but evidently I did not stir any thoughts in her.

So my life was empty and sterile, simple, and meaningless—just like the life of most of the university professors in the country. Sometimes, I wondered if it would not have been better to stay in the United States, like my friend Pierre, teaching the psychology of learning in Alabama or in South Dakota, and publishing articles in the APA journals.

Then, one morning, the newspaper brought the news that the government had been overthrown and replaced by a military junta. This was not such alarming news since it happened almost every day in many Third World countries. I looked at the news with a certain indifference, while I thought of dressing and leaving for the university. But this time it had not happened in Bolivia or in Zambia but in Panama, a few blocks from my house. I could almost say right in front of my nose.

The dictators could go to hell as long as they would leave me to my mediocrity and simplicity. Frequently, in one Third World country or another, a government collapsed and the military took over, causing world wide scandal and general embarrassment. The law of the fittest, social Darwinism, the weapons, dominated everywhere. Deep down it really did not bother me in the least. Hopefully the dictators would be crushed. In the end they had looked for it with their messianic fantasies and their need to be showy, to be in the newspapers, causing the United States' president to lose sleep....

"David, you're wanted on the phone," said one of the professors just as I was entering my office. I was reading the latest copy of the *American Psychologist* and wondering why the American journals had rejected the last three articles that I had submitted for their approval. They were modest and simple investigations, from the Third World, but to me they were important, anyway....

"Yes? Professor González of Central University speaking."

When the voice on the other end of the phone asked me to come to the Palace I really could not understand what it meant. Me?

To the presidential Palace? But what had I done? What crime had I committed?

"It's an order, Doctor. We'll be waiting at the door to take you to the General."

Luckily, by the grace of God—or Mother Nature—us introverts express neither our emotions nor our fear. When I arrived at the Palace, I was received by an aide who led me through a series of hallways and rooms. I was told to wait, the General would see me shortly. Hours and hours went by and the General did not arrive. Also, according to what little I had read in the morning paper, the government had been overthrown by a MILITARY JUNTA (in capital letters) and not by a general (in small letters). It was hot. I read the magazines and a couple of foreign newspapers that were in the waiting room. I kept wondering why the APA journals did not accept articles by psychologists from the Third World. The solution was to found a better journal that would not accept articles by psychologists from the First World.

"Doctor González, you're next."

The door opened and I saw a large room which had an enormous desk at the other end. A man of undefinable age was sitting in a big chair with the national flag behind him. Everything was solemn and ridiculous. There was a rug that ran from the door to the chair close to the enormous desk where this man was sitting. The aide accompanied me the whole time.

"Thank you, leave us alone," said the man behind the desk to the palace aide, when we were in front of him.

"As you wish, General."

I looked at him. He was a young man with very black hair and fine features. He had sparkling, intelligent eyes, unusual for a general of a *coup d'état* who overthrows the constitutional government in a Third World country. He was impeccable dressed and had the hands of an intellectual, and a serious but kind look.

"Sit down, Doctor."

Obviously I obeyed the order and kept quiet.

"You don't recognize me, do you?"

I really did not, but I did not know what to say. Besides, my score for social intelligence is quite low and I give the impression of being a perfect idiot. Of course, I should have said that I recognized him.

"We met a couple of years ago at a party. We talked about psychology and behaviorism. My name is Martin Luther King."

I was not immediately able to register the respective information so I made a stupid face. I think I always make stupid faces but at this moment I made an even stupider one than ever.

"I've called you to be my advisor. To convert a dream into reality that you and I will carry through, the dream of changing human history, of setting the world on a different and startlingly new course. Would you like a drink? Aide, come here!" he called. "Bring Doctor González and me a double whiskey, Johnny Walker, Black Label."

"You can't imagine the terrible state the country is in; this is why we, the forces in command, must act and help to reestablish order. The country is in bad shape; there is misery, inflation, unemployment, terrorism. Now there will be none of this because the five os us on the Military Junta have decided to put law and order where chaos formerly prevailed."

The conversation lasted several hours. I drank my whiskey and listened to what the General had to say. It was strange and fascinating. I felt as if I were on another planet. This man talked with vigor and conviction, with an energy that charmed me. I have never really been a strong man and have never been able to convince anyone of anything. That is why I have such admiration of strong people.

"We're going to change the world, to make a new country, to throw the 'gringos' out, to make a new Panama. I want you to be my personal advisor. I want us to use behavioral psychology in order to create a perfect society, to modify man, to change history. I want you to join me and help me, so that we can bring into being what Skinner couldn't do in *Walden Two*. Have you read *Walden Two,* Dave? It's about a vacational colony, a farm in the center of the United States where people work little and have a lot of free time. We're going to make a *Walden Three,* a new world, here in the tropics, in the middle of the palm trees and the heat, near the sea. Yes, it will have universal repercussions and it will help to change the course of history. We'll carry through the greatest dreams of humanity, with your help, you and I, David and Martin."

I drank my fourth whiskey and looked at him. The more I drank, the less able I was to talk. My God, how awful! I wanted to tell him that it was wonderful but impossible, because the Military Junta (with capitals) was made up of five men, but he was only one of them, and who knows what the others thought of the potentialities of Skinner's psychology for changing the world. I wanted to tell him that Skinner himself was discreet and reasonable, that he took social parameters seriously, while in the tropics the Negro dictators like him ... anyway, God had not given me the gift of gab and although I wanted to say a lot, in the end I said nothing. People maintain they like the way I keep quiet and listen. This to me is not a quality but a defect and it hurts me a lot. I do not say anything because I am not able to say anything. But at times people consider that qualities are defects and defects are qualities.

"We're going to make a perfect society, Dave. We're going to modify social behavior, plan human behavior, change child raising practices, reform the delinquents and change the educational system. Science has never been taken seriously, psychology has never been given an opportunity. The day has come. Today, the first of August. We're together. And the world's going to change."

I had my fifth whiskey and felt some strange pains in my head and back. It was around eleven o'clock and I had never gotten drunk so early. My friend felt just fine.

"David, take me seriously. We're going to do great things. I only want you to be sincere. Are you with me?"

"Yes Sir, I'm with you," I said, although I did not know what I was saying or the implications this would have.

CHAPTER 4
THE NEW GOVERNMENT

Revolutions are generally full of changes in plans, reforms and counter reforms. Many things are done by trial and error and plans already under way are altered. The Military Junta that had overthrown the legitimate constitutional government was at the same time "relieved" of its duties and replaced by only one of its members: Martin L. King. I think this implied a kind of internal *coup d'état*. My friend overthrew his companions of the dictatorship and sent them into exile. What actually happened is something that never was really known, and probably never will be.

What is known is that the other four members of the Military Junta asked for political asylum and went to Mexico. King stayed on as a 'strong man" and the only ruler of the country.

The newspapers did not comment very much on this change in power, as if they had not really understood very well what was happening. The new tropical dictator appeared on the front pages of the press, sometimes serious and sometimes smiling, alone or with his family, accompanied either by his five children or by his wife. He had a young-looking face, his hair was very black—even though some years had gone by and should have left him with some silver strands—and had the slim aspect of a man who worries about his figure and keeps in shape by doing exercise and controlling his eating habits.

After that first meeting at the time of the Military Junta, we met many more times and King explained exactly what he wanted me to do, how he thought we could change the country, applying the principles of behavioral psychology to social problems, what my role would be in this important transformation, and what he expected of me. I hesitated before accepting his proposal because I was frightened by his self-sufficiency, his impulsiveness, his paranoia, and his alcoholism. He drank and talked a lot. He had too many plans, too many ideas, and it seemed there was not enough time to do all he wanted.

First and foremost, it was necessary to attain an absolute government, the loyalty of the army and of the people. Next, the economic situation which was really chaotic had to be improved. Reforms in education, criminology and in other possible areas were planned for a later date. Or rather he wanted me to do everything with the help of Skinner and his rats. Without a doubt, it was quite a serious and complex problem!

First there was the problem of the North American influence on the country. The United States had interests in many Third World countries, and, politically, ours was one of the most important. The United States did not like dictators with messianic ideas. How was the new government going to handle this matter? Was it going to establish cordial relations with Washington and go on tolerating North Americans in the Canal zone? Or, alternatively, was it going to declare war and insist that they pack up their things and leave?

I did not know what would happen and I do not think anybody

had it very clear, not even my "friend" the dictator, president, strong man, or whatever we should call him. Anyway our relationship with the Colossus of the North was one of the first things that had to be solved.

"You've all the power you want, you can do things your way, change, reorganize, modify the behavior of man and society. Convert the country into the Walden Three we've already talked about. It won't just be a vacational colony like Walden Two but rather a real country. This is your chance to make the behaviorists' dreams come true: by controlling the environment completely. You can consequently control human behavior. It's an opportunity no intelligent man could afford to miss.

"I won't be able to work alone. I'll need people from this country and also some foreign technicians. I think we'll have to import experts from the United States."

"Of course, all you want! You can employ all the advisors you need. But it must be made clear that they'll be your assistants, merely acting in their capacity as technical advisors in the work that you're going to do. All the major decisions, the policies, the important responsibilities are in your hands. You're the boss. Do you agree? Whom did you have in mind?"

"Well, let's see, there're a series of students and followers of Skinner that have worked on socially important problems. For example, Keller has done much on individualized education and I think we could bring him. There are people in Kansas, in Rochester, and at Harvard who have worked on educational reform. The same is happening in other areas, for example, in economics, health and social planning, and the design of cultures."

"Bring them all. Let's offer them ideal conditions, magnificent salaries and especially the possibility of transforming Walden Three into a real state, thanks to the fact that we've the political and economical power of the country."

"For example, Holland, Ulrich, Staats, Azrin, Kazdin, Ayllon, Wolf . . . I don't know who else. Keller was even in Latin America before, and so was Bijou. We can invite them to collaborate with us. I think there may be ten experts altogether that could collaborate in designing a new society."

"They'll all collaborate with you but the decisions will be only yours. Ten people, that's fine. All of them from the United States. Is there no one from England or Russia, or even better, from

Cuba? You know I'm greatly attracted to the socialist system and I think Cuba could teach us a lot. Our Walden Three will follow a left-wing philosophy. It will be a socialist country in which the ideas of Marx and Lenin would form the ideological frame of reference and the experimental analysis of behavior would constitute the technological framework."

"The students of the Central University believe that behaviorism goes hand in hand with fascism and is against socialism."

"They're a bunch of ignorant citizens," objected Martin, 'There's nothing in behavioral analysis that relates it to either the right or the left. It's a science, a technology, a series of highly valuable instruments. It's neither a philosophy nor an axiology. I'll propose the ideology, the conceptual framework. Humanism will be our guide. We're going to help people do away with illiteracy, misery, superstition, children's diseases. We're going to make a new country. You get the tools and I'll devise the major policies and our goals."

I was very surprised that the psychologists to whom I wrote, ten in all, were interested in my proposal of coming to the Third World to collaborate with a Negro dictator of a tropical country in the creation of a new society with the help of psychology. None of them refused to come. They all asked for more information but ended up accepting my proposal. In a few months, I had here in the city the most select group of operant psychologists in the world. A dinner Martin gave them—whom they all called Mr. President—seemed more like a meeting of the executive committee of the twenty-fifth Division (experimental analysis of behavior) of the American Psychological Association. They all accepted the offer to collaborate with me. They all thought it was a magnificent idea. It was not necessary to offer them either exorbitant salaries or extraordinary conditions; it was just enough just having the opportunity to make a Walden Three, in a developing country and to have the liberty to apply their principles.

We started working right away. I had the title of Presidential Advisor, and was a kind of minister without portfolio but with a lot of power. The President eliminated the Congress from the very beginning, both the House of Representatives and the Senate. He appointed commissions on health, education, public works, science, foreign relations, etc. instead of ministers. He told me a thousand and one times that the coordinators of these commissions should always obey me and should follow the indications of the Group of Ten: that is my advisors on educational, legal, economical and all other matters.

Our work was exciting and difficult. We had to import many more people and each important psychologist brought his own team of collaborators, asked for endless offices, a large budget, assistants, bibliographical material, statistic and computer services. They spent money like water. The experts came and went, asked for data, materials, collaborators that could go around the country gathering statistics, and all this cost a lot. I was not used to this flow of money and I was worried that Martin—Mr. President—would be concerned about this tremendous outlay.

In order to reform education or the penitentiary system, for example, we needed to train hundreds of people how to use the new principles of experimental analysis of behavior. We had to buy tons of plastic tokens for the "token economy," bonds, recording sheets. We had to buy closed-circuit television sets, camaras with unidirectional vision, computers to process all the information. The Group of Ten which was made up of the top operant psychologists in the world, were very interested in research. It was necessary to plan and carry out experiments, to follow through and prove the efficiency of a method, to organize and select the most effective strategy. The country was boiling, not only with heat but also with plans and optimism. Nobody worried about the enormous expenses, except me.

Mr. President was very involved in foreign affairs which culminated in an encounter with the United States. Either they leave the country or Panama would destroy the Canal! Tension grew and grew, it became unbearable. Mr. President went to the United Nations, came back and spent days in meetings, polemics and intricacies, and I really had no idea how it would turn out. Curiously, in the end, the North Americans pulled out of Panama. They left in peace, without firing a single shot. They left to build another canal, more modern and functional, more adapted to the times than the Panama Canal. Although it obviously would have been more appropriate to construct this new canal in Panama, they planned to build it in Colombia or Nicaragua. But they were fed up with the problems of tropical dictators and preferred to show their good-heartedness and leave. Anyway, the canal was almost useless, it was obsolete by now and a bigger and more modern canal was urgently needed. The best thing the United States could have done was to free themselves of the problem, to leave Panama with grace and give the world an image of prudence, fairness and respect for her southern neighbors. In reality, what they did was to free themselves of an enormous headache and leave with their heads held high.

Panama was now a country without foreign domination and with a group of top quality international experts who, provided with an adequate budget, really wanted to work for change. This was the situation when we started our great social reform: the construction of Walden Three.

CHAPTER 5
THE CHILDREN FIRST

The commission of experts, the so-called Group of Ten, was with us for two years. Then they left and were replaced by scientists and technicians from Panama. During these two years they did many things, organized commissions, outlined major plans and drew up important policies.

Each working group—the recreation, the economy, or the child raising group—wrote a report that usually had hundreds of pages. Here the problem in question was analyzed, along with its possibilities for a solution, the way of handling the various alternatives, the expenses, the chronogram of activities. The commission passed the project on to me to be read and revised and I sent it on to Mr. President. Sometimes I made a few corrections in order to adapt the ideas of the commission in question to the tropical reality and the Third World, and other times, I rewrote some parts. Martin read each document conscientiously and commented on it in detail to me. I do not know how he found time to do it! He read everything, asked a lot of questions, got together several times with me and with the commission of experts. His capacity for work was really extraordinary, enviable. I have never known another tropical dictator who works so much, who takes the task of improving the life of his people so seriously.

"We can do this because we have political, military and economical power," said Mr. President. "Everything's in our hands: industry, the army, commerce, the press. Our government is totalitarian and autocritical, for this I'm criticized in international circles. But this is the only way we can reform the country. Imagine, Dave, what the procedure would be like for handling our reform if the country was ruled by a Congress! Then there would be legislative bodies that would give their opinion and their judgment on each one of our ideas. Years would go by, many years, before we would be able to introduce even one reform. This is the enormous failure of democracy. I think it was Churchill who ascertained that democracy was a very bad political system, but that the other alternatives were still worse. Okay, I agree with him completely."

"The commission on education considers that—"

"Excuse me, for interrupting, Dave. Someday I'll be leaving and will give the power back to the people. We'll have elections. Once the reforms are firmly established and when we have the New Man in a New Country in a New Era, I'll be able to leave. I think twenty years will be enough. We'll then have a new generation born under my leadership, men and women educated to make their own decisions, to have mutual respect, and to cooperate. The social planning of our world will have long started and won't be able to turn back."

I thought to myself: twenty years! These tropical dictators always have big plans and end up failing in two or three years; usually the pressure groups finish them off; at other times they simply accumulate enough money to take off and live in Europe, using the checking account they have secretly maintained in a Swiss bank.

But Martin was not one of these. He was more like a visionary with messianic fantasies. A different man, who, although having grandoise ideas, was intelligent and reasonable in his way of using them. Making changes has always been talked about, but the ones who have talked about it never had the political power to actualize such changes. Martin was a kind of philosopher-ruler, just like the ancient Greeks and Romans wished to have; I think it was Marcus Aurelius who talked of this.

"We make a magnificent working team. You plan, design, organize social changes. I put them in operation. We're something like the philosopher-ruler of ancient times, but in two people: you're the philosopher and I'm the ruler."

It was quite a coincidence that we should both think of the same thing at exactly the same time.

"It's impossible to find both in the same skin, that's why a philosopher-ruler as one person is a myth, impossible to obtain. But as two people, with defined roles, with distinct positions, thinking of the well-being of our people and in changing the world. . . ."

"Sure. I think the changes will be a success. Look, I have here the project on preschool education which I consider very important. Other programs are also revised, such as the ones on recreation and on economy."

"We'll begin with kindergarten education. First the children," King said.

"It's quite an extensive project which involves the education of the parents, diffusion of innovations, discipline problems, continuous education, prenatal hygiene and many other things. It starts from the moment of planning to have a child and continues until the child grows up and integrates into the society as a useful citizen, with a specific job and an adequate repertory of useful and adaptive behaviors."

"It would be the process of socialization."

"Yes, of course, in a broad sense. This project is related to the others, firstly with the family planning project which is one of the cornerstones of the economy and of our social reconstruction. It's important that each couple should plan their family, that they have their children when they're economically and psychologically prepared."

"Psychologically. Because the economy is going to change a lot; remember that I want to abolish money once and for all."

"Well, look. . . . It's not that easy. No society has done it; In reality, the kibbutz in Israel is the only experimental society that doesn't use money. What we should do is balance the salaries, give free health and educational services, etc. But let's go back to the children. When a couple decides to have a child, they go to the closest health center where they undergo medical and psychological examinations. There are so many hereditary diseases. Even alcoholism seems to have certain factors of genetic predisposition."

Martin looked at me strangely but did not make any comment.

"People with genetic problems," I continued "can get married but not have children. Sex, matrimony, living together, reproduction and conservation of the species are very different things. People tend to confuse them. To get married is one thing, to have children is another. Everyone should be allowed to get married if they want to, but not everyone should have children."

Although I had carefully read this reform program, it seemed very harsh when I stated it verbally: Spartan.

"If they want children they can adopt them. We're going to organize the adoption system very well, since every child needs a home, and some parents can take care of another's child with the same love as if it were their own. Of course, before giving them the child, they will have to undergo the appropriate training. We all have to learn to be parents, this isn't something that's automatically known, through God's will. . . ."

Since the concept of 'God' was not to have a place in the new Walden Three, I though it important to control my language and avoid vernacular expressions, those that one says without thinking. Morality and order were not to be based on God but on human and social ethics; but then, this was another project that we had fought to organize without much success. It was not easy to plan the ethics and morals of the new society, but this had to be done as soon as possible, since these and the ideological problems were at the base of the other reform programs.

The analysis of the project on early education and socialization took a long time. Mr. President raised various objections, made changes, and it was necessary to return the plan to the respective commission for further study and reform. Finally, a new version was attained which was more acceptable for everyone involved.

It included family planning, free medical and psychological services, information and training centers for mothers, free day-care centers for young children, part-time jobs so mothers could work without leaving their children, if possible at home or nearby; prenatal hygiene, early stimulation of newborn babies, involvement of the father and other members of the family in child raising, specialized training for women to become "substitute mothers," to care for the children in day-care and adoption centers.

Formal education started very early in the child's life. We believed that the child could learn to read and write at four or at least at five, if the proper methods were used. We had to develop basic skills and input repetoires, through environmental stimulation. Behavioral changes were achieved by modifying the environment. The other children would serve as the models and as the basis of socialization. Usually in traditional Western societies, child rearing is left exclusively to the family, and neighbors and everyone else are excluded. Here, in this new society that we were going to form, the other children would have a lot to do and child rearing would be collective.

The substitute mothers played a tremendously important role in the whole process. It was curious to see how for many women this was a perfect job, they worked with love and dedication, with true interest, and obtained magnificent results. They were women full of love but with no one to give it to, as either they had never had their own children or if they had, they had already left home. For them, being a substitute mother was a perfect job.

With the mothers, we stressed how important it was to talk to their children, hug them, hold them, kiss them, give them a lot of affection and security; to listen to what the child had to say and take him seriously; to keep the promises made to him. Corporal punishment was completely abolished; Mr. President even passed a law which stated that it was a crime to punish a child physically; a guilty parent would go to jail for one to three years.

In place of corporal punishment we explained in detail other ways to form behavioral patterns and socialize the child. The withdrawal of affection and privileges both became punishment techniques; the child also had to respond for his deeds and pay the price: he would lose a token for each inappropriate action, and if he did not have the adequate amount of tokens at the end of the day or week, he could not watch television or go to the movies, or even go out.

Socialization emphasized positive methods. Reinforcement and reward were constantly given but only in accordance with the response. The application of these reinforcement programs to everyday life was explained on television, radio, in public conferences, in pamphlets that were distributed freely throughout the whole country. Since illiteracy abounded, it was necessary to go to remote regions in the country, talk with the mothers, explain to them that they had no right to torment their children, and show them other alternatives in child raising. The initial reaction was very negative, one of skepticism and aggression, since the government was interfering in the private life of the people and was opposing the ancestral wisdom with which the peasant mother had raised her children for so many generations. But, later on, when they discovered that the system of points and tokens really worked, that it was easy to apply and very effective, and that corporal punishment only achieved temporary effects and a series of unrecommendable secondary consequences (like the child's fear and hatred of the parent who punished him), then slowly the reforms were accepted. The day came when the mothers commented with great enthusiasm on how they had gained changes in their children's behavior. They all agreed that the new system improved their own lives, saved them time, was more effective than the traditional alternatives and taught the child responsibility and order. In this aspect of child rearing, the program had great success, and spread like wildfire.

I wrote a small book in which all the principles and fundamentals of behavioral analysis applied to child rearing and socialization of children were explained. It was a clear and simple manual, adapted to the standard mentality of mothers of the tropics. It was called *The Formation of the New Man,* a showy title and a bit ridiculous, but Mr. President wanted it. I would have preferred to call it *Between Parents and Children,* which finally was left as the subtitle. The government printed 100,000 copies, which were given away to parents, teachers, substitute mothers, school administrators, governing bodies of health centers, doctors, nurses, psychologists and social workers.

In the book the reform of the socialization programs was planned in detail, firstly in emphasizing the role of the family and of other socializing agents. It demonstrated how we were carrying out a social experiment, never before undertaken on such a large scale, on a national level. The experiment would bear fruit in the long run and was designed with care and accuracy, without leaving anything unforeseen, at least relatively speaking since social phenomena are very complex with countless variables which are difficult to control. This experiment would have to be evaluated, and from this evaluation, changes in each case would be made.

The book also stated that education begins when a couple decides to have a child and continues throughout the process of conception, prenatal development, birth, the so important and neglected early infancy period, the preschool stage, primary and secondary school, and occupational training. In education there were many ideological and philosophical parameters that we were trying to make clear in order to submit them for the consideration of the people. A humanistic outlook was deemed the principal and most important guideline, a kind of behavioral humanism in which right was considered what was right for man and wrong what was wrong for man. It was not really an axiological absolutism but a new kind of humanism that took into account the cultural and historical relatively of events.

I think this ideological part of the book was the weakest since philosophy had never been my strong point. The psychological parts were much better. The explanation of the simple reinforcement schedules (fixed-ratio, variable-ratio, fixed-interval, variable-interval) as well as the multiple, concurrent, conjunctive ones, etc., was, I think, quite well done. Practical examples were given in all the cases. The book contained recording sheets, taught how to make simple and multiple base lines, how to make behavior records and to group them into categories. When talking of reinforcement, the importance of the contingency of its application was insisted upon; physical, symbolic, social, and internalized reinforcements were also mentioned. We were looking for a psychologically adult and mature man who would work under the unique reinforcement of his own satisfaction, and with the security of acting in accordance with the goals of the new society.

Discipline was planned on the basis of explanations given to the children and, obviously, on the basis of reinforcements. The importance of reasoning with the child, of explaining to him the causes and consequences of things, was insisted upon. Obedience should spring naturally from within the child and he should want to do what he had to do. I had to reflect upon such conditioning for, at least, a couple of weeks, but I think I finally explained it well. Obedience should come from within the child and not from external pressures, or from aversive consequences if he did not obey. Being within the same social context, the child and his parents should reach the same conclusions. There was no reason why discipline had to be a problem.

The child should have free time to play, express himself, talk, do whatever he likes, run around the patio, make a mess of the house, throw his toys on the roof. Of course, he would have to put everything back in its place. I insisted a lot upon the expression of these emotions, upon the "freedom" (another bad word) of the child. It is generally believed that conditioning implies putting people in chains, without freedom and self-determination. I would like, on the contrary, to see freer and more spontaneous children who would talk, shout, express their own emotions, and have a happy childhood rich in experiences.

These new children, who liked to do what they had to do, would be happy and creative children whose potentialities the new society was going to develop. Since ours was an egalitarian society, there were no social classes (we were in the process of abolishing them) and everyone had to be able to reach the top, in the sciences, in the arts, in his capacity as a human being.

A practical norm in child raising was to ask the parents to dedicate at least an hour a day to their child. I gave this norm the name of "Little Peter's hour" like the name proposed by a distinguished Panamanian psychologist. The "Little Peter's hour" was planned within the daily activities program, in the same way that the eating, sleeping and working hours were planned. During this hour, the parents should talk with, and listen to the child, and plans should be made together. The purpose was to socialize the young child, and to convert him into a human being through interaction with other humans (the so-called process of "humanization"); it was not necessary to teach him anything specific, only to be with him. I think that the "Little Peter's hour" was a great idea and I hope they have given it the importance that it deserves.

CHAPTER 6
THE CALENDAR REFORM

One of the projects that arose directly from Mr. President was the calendar reform. He, himself, wrote the project and passed it on to me, so that I would afterwards share the idea with the Group of Ten.

"Panama is a beautiful country," Martin said, "one of the most important countries in the world. The fact that two oceans touch our shores, that we have the largest transoceanic canal, and that we are a mixture of races—the cosmic race of Vasconcelos—makes us the heart of the planet. It's a marvelous country which I love dearly. It's time Panama taught the world something new and important, like our experiment in social reform, based on socialist ideology and on the technology of scientific psychology. Within this reform an aspect that interests me is the reform of the months, days, hours, the working days and the vacation season. I want us to adopt a new calendar in Panama and then submit it to the United Nations where they may consider it for adoption throughout the world.

In Martin's project, there were to be ten months instead of twelve, each one with thirty-six days. Each month was to be named after a great historical figure rather than a Greek or Roman God. Martin presented a long list of famous men so that we could select the ten names to be given to the months of the year. Each week was to have six days instead of seven and each day bore the name of a great figure.

The hours of the day changed and instead of saying "five in the morning" for the hour when the sun rose every day, it was called "one"; from there one started counting the twenty-four hours of the day. With the new schedule one would start working at three instead of eight in the morning, the time we now started.

There were not really any astronomical-type reforms, so to call Martin's project a calendar reform did not make much sense. But he always liked grand ideas and that is why we preferred to keep on talking about the "calendar reform" in the meetings of the Group of Ten where the project was exhaustively analyzed. There was an interesting and strange point regarding the day off, our Sunday. Each month had thirty-six days and was made up of six weeks, each of these of six days (six times six is thirty-six). The project proposed that people should work five days each week and rest one. The interesting point was that this day of rest varied: not everyone was free on "Sunday"; some groups were free on "Monday," others on "Tuesday," etc. In this way the society was not paralyzed as in other countries on days off. There were two ways of doing this: either by professions and jobs (Physicians on "Monday," bricklayers on "Tuesday," etc.) or by city zones: zone number one (for example, postal zone one) was free on Monday, zone 2 on Tuesday, etc. Both alternatives were in the project but Mr. President made it clear that he preferred the second one, in which the day off depended on the city zone; this was, of course, for practical reasons.

"The French during the Revolution had carried out a similar reform regarding the names of the months, my friend Mercedes, one of Mr. President's advisors, told me. Mercedes, who was somewhere between thirty and forty years old, was a teacher in a kindergarten, and very cultured.

"I think this reform was a failure," I said.

"Yes, that's for sure, and although the names of the months and the days are silly conventionalisms, the custom already exists; there's a written history that can't be changed. For example, if America was discovered October 12, 1492, we can't now say that it was the month of Goethe 1492. I hope it won't occur to Mr. President to change the years! That would be awful, David. You, who are the President's pet child, convince him that it's an absurd idea. Imagine a more radical change in the calendar, such as that history begins the day Martin L. King took power in this small equatorial republic and decided to change the world. Everything else was 'before' the New Era. Can you imagine the mix-up in history books?"

"Mercedes, you're right, but I think that Mr. President has never thought of changing the years. The idea of the months and weeks doesn't seem too absurd to me and I must confess that one day off a week according to one's occupation or city zone is very appealing."

"A ten-month year, a thirty-six day month and a six-day week in which five are working days and one is a holiday ... Hmm ... the problem is that Panama doesn't exist in a vacuum, and a reform like this is absurd unless it is accepted throughout the world, which is not going to happen. There's another point: the ten months give the year three hundred sixty days, so your President friend has five days left over (and in leap years six days). What does he propose doing with these extra days?"

"I guess collective vacations, although this really goes against his policy of having the country functioning at all hours, including Sundays. I guess those extra days will be for some special purpose. But now I remember! It's in the project. Didn't you read it all? Those days will be for meditation. It seemed very strange to me when I read it. It says that we would have a kind of "intellectual retreat" (just like the monk's spiritual retreat), to plan the coming year, to weigh up the activities, accomplishments and failures of the past year. It would be a period of inventory and national evaluation. Martin insists people don't think, don't plan, don't have time to speculate. According to the new calendar there are five days extra; five 'unattached' days put aside at the end of the year just for the purpose of thinking. I would guess that the people will take advantage of this 'transcendental meditation' to go on vacation to the beach rather than reflect upon the past year or the one to come."

"Yes," observed Mercedes. "In any kind of scientific program it's important to evaluate the results, to make permanent and critical evaluations, to have feedback in relation to what is happening. If this is a scientific society, and even more important, if it's based on the experimental analysis of behavior, this evaluation is vitally important."

"At any rate, it won't be simple meditation at home. I sympahtize with people who examine their conscience daily, who meditate in the privacy of their home and carefully plan the next day. In Panama we're going to do it on a national level! I think the most appropriate thing to do for these five days of the year is to organize discussion groups at every level, in the urban zones, in the country, in the factories, in order to study the government reports, to criticize the obtained results and to plan the next stage. In this way our people will be actively participating in the process of change. It's very important that everyone should consider himself part of this immense social reform, that he should become involved in the improvements that are being achieved, and that people don't feel it's merely something that's being forced upon them by Mr. President and his advisors."

"My dear, you talk with contagious enthusiasm. Anyone would say you're vitally involved in the psychological and social transformation of the country."

"Of course, obviously I am. Usually I don't talk much, but you inspire me, Mercedes."

We laughed for a while and later discussed the list of great figures that Martin had proposed as names for the months and the days of the week. It included such philosophers as Socrates, Plato and Aristotle from "this side," the western culture; Confucius and Lao Tse from the "other side"; statesmen such as Churchill and De Gaulle; warriors such as Attila; scientists such as Einstein and Newton; writers such as Thoreau and Shakespeare; religious leaders of distinct creeds, such as Jesus and Buddha; people of yesterday and today, both men and women, but predominantly men.

"History has been made by some 100 men and a dozen women," Martin answered when I commented on the scarcity of women on his list. "After all, I've included the greatest women of history such as Catherine of Russia, Queen Victoria of England, Marie Curie, and the Bronte sisters. I hope we'll have at least one woman in the final list. We have to reduce the list to sixteen names! Ten for the months and six for each day of the week.

"They tried to do something similar in the French Revolution, as did Comte later on."

"Comte's list of names is simply stupid, just like the ridiculous names given to the months of the year by the French revolutionaries. But we aren't going to do anything like that. We're selecting the most outstanding people in history to baptize the months of the year and the days of the week. What's the most important thing this planet has produced? Without a doubt, her great men. They've made history and changed the world."

I did not want to discuss that the historians of today prefer to say that the *zeitgeist* or the spirit of time, is the cause of social change and not the great men; that history is, apparently, less than what the profane philosophers of history think, that discoveries and inventions are inevitable. Man's role in shaping history is apparently less important than the abusers of the subject suggest.

"We're going to eliminate Mars, Venus, Juno and other gods from the calendar, and put in their places men of flesh and blood, who fought to better the life of their travel companions and to decipher the mysteries of the universe."

The subject of the names of the months provoked various discussions among the Group of Ten and the different commissions. The discussions were not taken very seriously since deep down nobody believed that Mr. President would dare change the calendar. But he did. He changed it, even though my friend Mercedes insisted that a change like that was impossible unless it was done worldwide, given that a country did not exist in a vacuum . . .

"For example, think of travel," Mercedes said to me, "flight schedules are made for the whole world, and the days and times are listed. Now, how are they going to fit us in? Here the flights won't arrive on Friday at 11:00 a.m. but on the day of Plato at the hour of six. Impossible, simply impossible!"

Mr. President gave the months names but had the good sense not to do the same with the days of the week. I do not know who made that suggestion. The days of the week were now letters, from A to F: Monday was day A, Tuesday day B, etc. There was a transition period in which both the old and new terminology were used, and the need to learn the new terms was particularly emphasized.

Since we, his advisors, were not able to reach an agreement, Mr. President determined the final list of names for the months of the year. Everyone was dissatisfied by his choice but it, at least, ended the interminable and senseless discussions. The names of the ten months were Lao Tse, Moses, Jesus, Socrates, Leonardo, Darwin, Marx, Marie Curie, Freud and Einstein.

"Too many religious leaders," commented Mercedes, "Too many scientists. There's no one from the Middle Ages. And who can convince me that Freud deserves to be there? You don't believe he does, do you?"

"Mr. President wanted to include Skinner, but that would have been too much. We're building a society based on Skinner's principles and on top of that we elevate Skinner to cosmic heights, substituting his name for a Greek god? No, Mercedes, we would be the laughing stock of the entire world. But it's all right to include Freud, he's an historical figure, a thinker with whom one may or may not agree, but anyway he's part of our civilization. I don't think the list is so bad. It includes different areas, people from various eras and countries, thinkers of distinct orientation, such as Marx and Jesus. No, I think Martin thought about it a lot before proposing the definitive list."

"You always defend him. In any case, whatever happens, I think we're going to be the laughing stock of the world for having had the audacity to change the calendar."

CHAPTER 7
WORK

Changing the length and the names of the months was something of nominal value that filled the front pages of newspapers all over the world but really did not have many immediate consequences. Nevertheless, the labor reform of taking one day off a week, depending on the city zone where one lived, did.

The capital city was divided into zones, as were all the other cities in the country. In all cases, they had to have numbers divisible by 6, one city had 18 zones, another 12, another 24. People took their day off without paralyzing the city which is what happened in the rest of the world during holidays. Here, in our new society, business did not stop, industries kept on working the whole time, one could always find a doctor or a dentist, it did not matter what day it was; if the dentist in our zone were on holiday, one just went to another zone. It was the same story if one wanted to buy a shirt or a pair of shoes.

The people liked this very much. It was new and unusual, it was attractive in that it was unknown. Only a few skeptical old people looked on the new system with distrust, sure that it would not work. For most of the population it was a reform that drew a lot of attention and was well accepted by the majority of the people.

Another aspect gave rise to greater misgivings: the complete reform of the labor system. The respective commission based itself on statistics and data from the Commission on Economy to propose a labor week with a flexible schedule. Everyone should work forty hours a week (five working days, normally of eight hours each), but they could organize these hours as they liked. One could work only four days instead of five as long as one could comply with the obligatory forty hours in these four days; in this case one would have the day off in one's city zone plus another free day of one's own choice.

It was difficult to organize the flexible schedules in the small companies with few employees. But in the larger ones this was easy to do if it were always planned in advance; secretary A does not come on Monday; B does not come on Tuesday, etc. In the companies with only one secretary, these changes were more complex and required reprogramming. In some places there was pressure to keep the five day week working eight hours each day. Furthermore, contrary to what one would think the employers had no difficulties in organizing their own flexible schedules.

When compiling the behavior records with all the norms of the case, using a multiple base line, it was found that Mondays and Fridays were the busiest days. In the new terminology, day A

(Monday) and day E (Friday, the eve of holiday F) were the most active. Therefore this had to be taken into consideration in the flexible schedules. Also there were certain hours which were busier than others, between ten and twelve in the morning in the old schedule (from five to seven in the new schedule, being hour one when the sun rose, which was five a.m. before). At this time, on A and E days, most commercial transactions, professional appointments, and other diverse activities were carried out. This also had to be born in mind while planning.

"I think that forty hours a week is excessive," said Martin in a meeting with the Labor Commission. "To work forty hours in routine and other such monotonous activities, which are the majority, is too much. For a worker or a secretary there is no time left for absolutely anything, except for working."

One of the experts on times and movements from the Labor Commission insisted that routine work, well-learned, with adequate lighting conditions and technology, was not a heavy activity, did not consume much energy, and such a person did not have to make many decisions. . . .

"What's left for this person? What will his life become? A worker is an extension of the machine he is handling. A secretary really is an extension of her typewriter and her filing cabinet. We want free and autonomous people, who don't have to work much and have a lot of time to dedicate to their children, to their mate, to arts and science and to cultivate their minds. The goal is a twenty-hour work week and not forty."

"All the reports from the Commission on Economy show that this is impossible, Mr. President."

"I know that. It's impossible *now*. I hope it won't be for very long. We must increase production which means we must work more, not cut the working day in half. I know, I know, I've read the project of the Commission on Economy, which, by the way, seems to me to have a lot of defects. I think the Commission on Economy is the weakest of all the commissions that make up National Planning."

"Are we failing because of the economy?" I asked timidly.

"We aren't failing at all! Everything is going fine. I don't accept criticism or reproach. The society is the greatest experiment attempted by man! The experiment most . . ."

Mr. President stopped talking when he noticed my serious and attentive face. I did not want him to repeat his sermon that we had already heard dozens of times in the past year.

But the truth was that some foreign companies had left the country and others threatened to follow suit. Various important capitalists had fled although they had not taken their factories nor the money invested in the country. It was sad to see that people did not understand the potentialities of the new system and preferred to go abroad and observe from afar the social changes without taking an active part in them.

But the economy marched forward, and, this phenomenon of the foreign companies leaving and the national capitalists trying to escape, had already been considered in the project outlined by the commission. Mr. President had not yet made any decision about his opponents, so whoever wanted to leave the country could do so without any problem; but they could not take their money or their companies.

"The work reform is psychological and economical," said one of the experts. "We base everything on the principles and laws of learning in order to motivate the workers, to stimulate them and control their output. We're interested in the extrinsic reinforcements, like money, and also in the intrinsic ones, such as personal satisfaction. The plan, in the long run, hopes to lay much less emphasis on the extrinsic motivations and much more on the intrinsic motivations. Although, as you know, we have to eat."

"Payment," continued another expert of the Labor Commission, "will be made on the basis of *reinforcement schedules*. Not haphazardly but contingently. The present schedules (when one is paid at fixed-interval reinforcement schedules, each fifteen or thirty days) will be substituted by the fixed-ratio schedules in which one will earn according to the work done. The person who works more, earn more. The work environment will be controlled and made as attractive as possible. The job should be pleasant and mean something for the person doing it. Work should be fascinating and not just a way to keep from dying of hunger. . . ."

"Or of boredom" added another expert.

"Exactly. People work for many reasons and we're going to make motivational programs that emphasize the positive values of work. An important aspect is the emotional support given by the group, since working is a *social activity;* we work with other people, and for other people. And the most important stimuli for human being come from other humans and not from material goods."

"When I was a student in the United States, the great importance the country gave to money had always shocked me. It was said that one worked almost exclusively for money. However, people who had enough money did not stop working, and the controlled studies carried out by industrial psychologists demonstrated that people work for a great number of reasons, money being only one of them, but not the most important. People work to give meaning to their lives, to keep busy, to acquire independence, status, and a sense of achievement; they work because they feel good with their workmates. They work to keep active, to be well accepted by their community; they work for many reasons."

"I want to clarify one point," the expert who had spoken before said, following his line of reasoning. "Different reinforcement schedules will be set up for different activities. I said before that we're going to emphasize the fixed-ratio rather than the fixed-interval schedules but what we're really going to do is design programs for each specific situation; most of the reinforcement schedules will be complex, multiple, conjunctive, interwoven, etc."

"And what about the extinction of money?" asked Martin impatiently.

"Yes, Mr. President, that's another chapter of the project. I think it will be difficult to abolish the use of money, and in many case, it hasn't been scheduled for the first five years. Later on, it may be possible."

"Five years! Too long, too long ... we should replace money with benefits for housing, health, education. ..."

"We've already made health and education free," I reminded him, "and we're offering housing at really ridiculous prices. One of the areas where we're investing more money, is in housing for the poor."

"Yes, I know. And I never suspected it would turn out to be so tremendously expensive to give a decent house to each family in need. Where on earth did all these people live before? Under a rock? Now they have a house or are in process of getting one and it's costing them practically nothing."

"It has cost us a lot, Mr. President. It's one of the projects that will have to be analyzed very carefully during the meditation days at the end of the year."

One of the most important achievements of the new government had been to get rid of unemployment which had been at a rate of eight percent before and even higher if we take underemployment into account. The new social system had given work to everyone, had created a lot of jobs in the government since the new plans required the help of an enormous amount of people for its implementation. Besides, the governmental posts at all levels, jobs were also created to discourage automation in factories and enterprises. It was of the utmost importance that everyone should have a job, so that the company would not count on modern and sophisticated technical equipment in which a machine does the work of ten or more men.

Where did the money come from to pay for these new jobs, especially the ones in the government? Would we not fall into the trap of capitalism and put currencies without reserves into circulation in order to pay so many new employees? I had read about the dilemma of unemployment-inflation and it frightened me a lot: if inflation is controlled, then unemployment increases, if unemployment goes down, inflation grows. We had chosen to terminate unemployment. Supposedly all these factors could be controlled by a centralized economy; at least that is what the Soviet books say in defending what we call "state capitalism" as opposed to individual capitalism.

There was no doubt that in such a planned and controlled society as ours, the economy had to be fundamentally in the hands of the government. Nothing could be left to chance. The economy was too important to leave it in the hands of the economists.

CHAPTER 8
CHINA OR THE USSR?

Nobody knows why the United States did not like anything that was happening in our country. They have always thought that they have to give an opinion on everything that is happening in each corner of the world, whether asked for it or not. The truth was that the United States government showed "profound concern" for the accelerated social changes that were taking place.

In a few years we had done away with unemployment, we had socialized medicine, almost wiped out illiteracy, had given everyone housing. That sounded bad, it sounded like communism. A terrible word. Besides, the government insisted that its frame of reference was either a kind of *socialistic humanism* or *humanistic socialism*. The North American companies had decided to leave the country, creating confusion and great disorder in the national economy. We were left almost bankrupt when the North American enterprises left. I, who had never really understood anything about economy, got an idea of the real power that money has in this world. We were left on the edge of an abyss, at the point of bankruptcy, and our social reform almost failed, just because the big capitalists of Wall Street suspected that our country could be converted into a second Cuba!

It seems that Moscow and Peking had the same idea as we had. In the span of a few months we received "unofficial" delegations from China and the USSR that wanted to visit the new social experiment of the Third World to see what was going on in our tropical country. The difference between this social reform and the others undertaken in various countries was that we based ours on *science,* especially on the science of human behavior. We believed that the revolution started in infancy, with the practices of child raising. We attached great importance to *psychological factors* in production, in taking social decisions, in the sense of commitment to the changes and the reforms. We wanted to change the family, sexuality, and work. It was a more profound, vital and longer-lasting revolution.

The delegation from China arrived first. It was composed of a dozen of very kind but impassive officials who left Peking for Panama by way of the United Nations. They stayed a while in New York and later arrived in Tocumen. Mr. President and his trustworthy colleagues, I being one, went to the airport to receive them.

"I don't know anything about China," Mr. President confessed to Mercedes, to Eduardo, who was in charge of communications, and to me. "I only know it's a gigantic country, where they speak Mandarin, and where they had a man like Mao, who had successfully transformed his huge country from the stone age to the atomic age in two decades. I also know that they quarrel with the USSR and consider that a Third World War is inevitable. Likewise, I know that their appreciation of Confucius and Lao-Tse is changing with the present government and that, in general, is not very positive. But Mao, he was a great man! It's incredible how a person like that could exist! I remember his struggles, his accomplishments, the way in which he organized the country. When China announced that they had the atomic bomb, everyone fell over backwards, just as when the USSR launched the first sputnik. Countries of peasants, poor and underdeveloped countries like China and the USSR should not be able to achieve such feats."

"Today, nobody considers them poor or underdeveloped," observed Eduardo. "On the contrary, they're two of the most industrially and technologically advanced countries in the world. They've undertaken social changes and they've showed them to the world at the opportune moment. I don't think their planning system has been equalled by any other country."

No one knew what to expect when the plane carrying the Chinese delegation was about to land. The Chinese arrived, spoke all the time in correct Spanish with a Caribbean accent—something that surprised us and pleased us very much.

We visited the schools, the factories and the health services with them. We showed them the housing projects, the plans for expanding industry, and we talked about the family reform. Mercedes wanted to tell them about the changes that were to be undertaken in more controversial and complex areas such as sexuality. But Mr. President remarked that the Chinese were known as puritans and would therefore think that we were all sexual libertines in the tropics, and that would spoil their visit. So we only showed them those accomplishments that could impress them—to *apantallarlos* as they say in Mexico. We did not show them the things that could disturb them. Oh, international politics!

They were very interested in the calendar reform, and also in the different vacation periods of the year and the day off on distinct days of the week, depending on the city zone where one lived.

"We find," explained Eduardo, our expert in communications, "that people move in a relatively limited circle, geographically speaking. Their children go to school not too far from home and they themselves go to a doctor or a dentist not too far from their home or work. Thus, residents in zone four, for example, can take their day off at the same time, including factories, professional services, schools and residences."

"The same happens with the annual vacation," he continued, "they're taken at different seasons of the year. Before, everyone went to the beach in December and the hotels couldn't accommodate so many people. The service was bad, and during this season the country was paralyzed. It was something like what happens in France and Spain during the month of August, when the people disappear from the cities and leave them to the tourists."

The Chinese smiled but did not say anything. Without a doubt, our social reform was centered around "unimportant" things from their point of view, like the family, the children, the psychological factors of work, and recreation. The big economical and ideological problems had not been explained to them. They would probably think that the social reform was incomplete and only had limited possibilities.

"The country works 360 days a year without any interruption. The ten months, each of six weeks, are fully occupied, and this had had very positive repercussions," I explained.

"And what about the five or six extra days of the year?" asked one of them, speaking Spanish as if he had been born in Panama, not in Peking.

"They're for meditation," I explained, feeling a little uncomfortable about this. "The people congregate in factories, schools, theaters, houses, and evaluate the year that's ending and make plans for the coming year. The government sends out reports each year on the achievements and the failures so the people can analyze them. . . ."

Martin looked at me and I noticed he did not want me to mention the fact that we had also had failures and that these were reflected in the annual reports.

"The meditation needn't be limited to the government reports," added Mercedes. "People can meditate on what they like, although we give them suggestions through our social communication system. We want the family to be together, so that they can talk, think a lot, solve their internal problems. In this period of meditation, a couple may decide to get married, another to get divorced, another to send their son to a special school. It's time for reevaluation, for introspection, and even for silence."

The health and education systems were similar to other socialist systems, and really the Chinese were not very interested in them either. In the last few meetings with the government's advisory group, a possible collaboration with Peking was vaguely discussed, to help bring the results of our revolution into the open, but nothing was settled. The Chinese left without promising anything great. I always thought that China would be very interested in having an American country that would depend on her and follow her ideological orientation. The USSR has Cuba, right next door to the United States. But China does not have anyone in America.

The visit from the Soviet delegation was longer and the people were more expressive. There were more questions, more meetings, more explanations. Among the Soviet experts who came were some men and women of Spanish descent who had migrated to the USSR after the Spanish Civil War and had settled there. Various Cubans also came.

One night when we had just visited a training center for substitute mothers, directed by one of the leading North American psychologists specializing in early stimulation—a center that had particularly attracted the Soviet's attention since they place a great interest on their own children in the USSR—Martin seemed tired and annoyed.

"I don't like the imperialism of the Cubans," he told me. "Look what they did in Africa. Look how Panama interests them. Now they want to play the "redeemers" of the Third World, and they dedicate themselves to "advising" guerrillas in Africa and Latin America. Their performance in Bolivia, in Angola, in so many other countries is really imperialistic and implies interference in the internal affairs of such countries. They want the revolution in Soviet style to spread throughout the world, with the same faith that the first Christians had when they spread theirs; they're the crusaders of the twentieth century, those Cubans."

"They've always been known as a hard-working and organized people. Whatever they do, they do it well. The Cubans who migrated to the United States or to Puerto Rico progressed quickly, they adapted to their new country and climbed up to important positions. They're industrious, serious and thrifty. They don't resembel the other people of the Caribbean in any way nor are they cast in the mould of the Latin American stereotypes."

"I don't know what they want from us. Their attitude is so seductive and beguiling and that makes me boil with rage. The Chinese, on the contrary, were more serious and discreet; they came to observe and I'm sure that soon I'm going to receive some well-structured program of technical help from them. These Russians and their Cuban friends are jabberers: they promise a lot and talk a lot. I believe the Russians, before coming to the Caribbean, weren't like that, but they've adapted to our geographical and cultural reality. I don't like them at all. I prefer the Chinese."

Both visits created tension among the members of the country's governing body. Our commission on Social Communication, presided over by Eduardo, a young and dynamic communications engineer who specialized in sociology, suggested that we should not inform the people of these visits since they were "unofficial." I thought it immoral to keep this information secret but Martin ended up agreeing to it. Information is dangerous. Knowledge is power, and we always ended up paying attention to what the experts told us. This was a scientific society. If the new science of social communication said that spreading the news about the visits of the Chinese and the Russians in the newspapers, radio and television, was going to create hopes and fears among the people, that it would have bad results, and that it was better not to mention these visits, then we were going to follow the advice.

"The Chinese never knew that the North Americans had landed on the moon, or that Nixon had visited China, until long after the events ocurred. It's an important principle of social communication to consider the *consequences* of handing out information," explained Eduardo.

I told myself that the freedom of the press and of information were human rights and that only totalitarian governments, of the extreme left or extreme right, suppress such rights. Were we headed that way?

The Chinese and the Russians sent polite letters of thanks and soon after, concrete plans arrived of economic and social collaboration. For China and the USSR, we were valuable prey, we were in the process of making great ideological decisions and they could "help" us to make them. For China it would be wonderful to have Panama in her orbit, now that the North Americans had abandoned the Canal and their industries had left, almost crippling the country economy.

On the other hand, the Russians could save us from the Chinese and the North Americans. After all, Cuba was an hour's flight from Tocumen and we always had great respect and admiration for the Cuban Revolution. If there was something that resembled the New Era that Martin was trying to establish in Panama, it was the Cuban Revolution from the beginning. Welcome to the Club!

The meeting of the entire Department of National Planning, presided over by Mr. President, lasted several hours. It was a tense and difficult reunion since we were making important decisions and no one knew how they were going to influence our future. The Commission on Economy considered that we could not survive alone, that the present world was interdependent—as Kissinger had said so many times—and that is why it was necessary to join with the Russians or the Chinese once we had left the North American orbit of influence. According to the Commission, the Russians offered better guarantees.

We had all studied the proposals from China and the USSR carefully. We had lost sleep thinking about the problem. I do not think everyone had stopped contemplating the profound implications of such a collaboration, and the dramatic change it was going to represent for our history and for our culture of not being pro-North Americans anymore and becoming pro-Soviet or pro-Chinese. It was a fact, that "alone" we could not survive in this complex and interdependent world of the last decades of the twentieth century.

I would have liked us to have become members of a great Latin American Alliance, of which Mexico or São Paulo would be the capital. But this common market had already failed dismally and the Latin American countries were separating more and more instead of uniting. I did not want to depend on Peking nor on Moscow, but on my Latin American brothers. But this was not the subject under discussion that tense morning, in the month of Darwin, at the sixth hour of the day. The decision was to whom we were going to sell ourselves: to the USSR or to China.

Suddenly the long speech Martin had been making, ended. He had talked for hours (in this way, he resembled Fidel Castro, he liked to hear himself talk although he was a terrible speechmaker). I had lost the thread of what he was saying. All of a sudden, I heard him exclaim:

"Neither Marx nor Jesus! Neither Lenin nor Mao. We're going to exist alone, We will have our own economy and our own system. We're not going to depend on China, on the USSR or on the United States. We'll be a social alternative, a different system, a new society that doesn't resemble anything that man has tried before."

Everyone talked and talked. Finally the discussion came to a close because it was quite late. It was past nine and we had to eat. Mr. President had not convinced all of the members of the Commission on Economy, but he had made a great decision: we were going to depend on no one. We were going to give a negative answer to the USSR and to China and survive alone. In spite of the fact that we all need others in order to exist. In spite of the economical and political interdependence of nations at this time.

CHAPTER 9
SOCIAL COMMUNICATION

The visits of the Chinese and Soviet delegations to the country brought up the discussion about the communication problem, the freedom of information, the role played by the radio, the television and the newspaper in the New Era.

Eduardo Cantón, who was very close to Mr. President and had collaborated most in the social revolution in progress, was in charge of the Commission on Social Communication. Eduardo, Mercedes, and I were without a doubt Martin's trustworthy colleagues and also his closest advisors. The Commission on social Communication, as it was called after many discussions, was tremendously important for the country and its new society.

Although the science of communication draws elements from sociology, psychology, the theory of information, and even systems engineering, it is a discipline with its own field and its own methodology.

"The psychological, behavioral, emphasis of the New Era of our history can be very important for this science and its application," explained Eduardo in a preliminary report sent as a work document to Mr. President.

The first thing the Commission on Social Communication did was to carry out an analysis of the content of the material published in the newspapers several months before the beginning of the New Era. They analyzed newspapers for and against the government, the serious and the yellow press. Also an analysis was made of radio and television transmissions, which included soap operas, songs, commercials and other relevant material. This served as a starting point for a complete and very transcendental reform of the communications media.

The results of this analysis were dramatic and awesome. The newspapers, radio and television transmitted, above all, news of crimes, scenes of violence and terror, and messages of a sexual nature in which the woman was nothing more than a seductive object of pleasure for the man. The commercials were simplistic and repetitive, and they attempted to ingrain on people's mind messages about the best shampoo, the store selling useless things for less than cost price, the most adequate way to have young-looking skin at 80 years old. The songs were ridiculous, always telling the senseless story of the woman who abandons her man for another. This message of abandonment and loneliness was repeated a thousand and one times in the songs, when in reality, at least in our Latin culture, it was the man who abandoned the woman (and not the other way around).

"It's curious to think that all the songs say the same thing," pointed out Eduardo, "The message is always the same. She leaves him plunged into loneliness and abandonment. "Tell her to come back, to come back now, time is flying and life is going by . . . " could be a synthesis of the message. It's repeated in practically all the songs from different countries and different cultural backgrounds. Argentinian, Mexican, Spanish, Venezuelan songs, always the same old story. It's curious isn't it?"

"You wanted to be a singer, didn't you?" I asked him indiscreetly."

"Well, man, that's not the point," he answered. "Yes, I wanted to be a singer and even made a couple of single records. It wasn't easy, there was a great deal of competition. Besides, I was interested in profound and philosophical themes, not in the simplistic and repetitive ballads. I could never have been successful as a singer because of my personality. That's why I studied engineering and did graduate work in sociology in the United States."

"But there are singers with a message, especially political, who have been very successful. Like Joan Baez for example who is still listened to, even though the years have gone by. Or Violeta Parra among the 'serious' singers," said Mercedes.

The three of us were sitting having coffee in my office, resting up from the day's work, informally discussing the task of the Commission on Social Communication.

"Have you ever heard that saying 'a song will never stop war?' I like it, it's the truth," I said.

"That's why it's necessary 'to sing just for the sake of singing not for worrying.' But, seriously, people's heads are full of those simplistic, repetitive, absurd messages, which have nothing to do with reality. The songs are damaging and take up a lot of time on the radio . . . and in people's minds. Once I read that the 'mind' is no more than its content; for modern man, as for Ibsen's Peer Gynt, personality is like an onion; when it's peeled there's nothing to be found underneath. The peelings are what he hears, what he reads, what he is taught, what others expect him to do, what he thinks that others think. . . . Finally, what is he? Nothing; like Peer Gynt, he's an onion."

"My soul is no more than its content," was a phrase coined by Hume" Mercedes remarked.

"Therefore, we must take care of the content. A person's mind is made up of criminal news, sexual fantasies of inaccessible, pneumatic bionic women . . . it's made up of a couple of sugary tunes that it repeats when it's alone, of advertising about things that it can't buy and really doesn't need. Our peasants receive messages in the newspapers about summer trips to Europe, about how to make millions of dollars just by investing cents, and about murderers who kidnapped a minister and received a fortune to free him, even though they tortured and killed him anyway; obviously the police were never able to apprehend them. This is what radio, television and the newspapers have to tell them. We're going to change all this, we're going to do it with the help of science."

"You've outlined the basic plan. Now you have to design and implement the cure. I don't envy you at all, man! It won't be an easy task."

To the man in the street it was strange that the radio was transmitting messages concerning health, education and life style. Soon, instead of the well-known commercials about the "best shampoo in the world," a message insisting that parents should talk to their children, should listen to them and treat them as friends, was to be heard; in this way the problem of the generation gap could be solved.

Another message was about contagious diseases, including venereal, and how to recognize them and prevent them from spreading. It gave detailed and simple information on biological aspects and their handling; it described symptoms, causes, what's known about them, and ended giving the addresses of the treatment centers in the city. All treatment was, of course, completely free of charge.

Another message spoke of labor and its relation to behavior. It was pointed out that work and love are the cornerstones of human life, even though love has been talked about much more than work. People need to be active, to be useful, to achieve goals. One should find that occupation which satisfies one and allows one to develop as a human being, and for this there are Orientation Centers in the city (such and such an address). Work must have meaning, be interesting and emphasize intrinsic motivations. One should not work only for money because this implies a nearsighted vision of life.

Such messges surprised the people at first but afterwards they began to take them seriously. There were messages about physical and mental health, order, discipline, entertainment. For the government (through the Commission on Recreation) free time and sports were highly important. Eduardo made it very clear that the Social Communication had no reason to make propaganda about the government; if the New Era was doing so marvellously well, as we all said, then what need was there for propaganda? The projects spoke for themselves.

Besides educational messages, the radio and television transmitted music, travel programs, history, plays and novels, but everything bore a message. The radio and television programs were integrated into the Government Division of Continuous Education. They emphasized the natural values and those of Latin America, but did not isolate them; the ultimate intention was to integrate them into an universal culture. Literary works of national authors—there were not many, unfortunately—were transmitted, where we attempted to outline our own values.

The air time dedicated to the traditional songs, meaning the romantic ballads transmitted for hours and hours by radio before the New Era, was reduced to ten percent. In order to fulfill the need for that type of melody, a group of composers were contracted to create songs with a social, philosophical, psychological message that would emphasize the national values and the importance of the New Era. The new songs, for example, were about the peasants who had migrated to the city only to die of hunger and become beggars or delinquents, and who finally went back to the country but under much better conditions than before; they told the story of a woman, Dolores, who was born in the slums, was a beggar, a flower vender and eventually became a schoolteacher. It proved in every case that one could better oneself instead of sitting around, weeping and feeling sorry for oneself.

"Maria begs for alms at the Cathedral," hummed Mercedes one afternoon when I entered her house without knocking. "Maria, Maria, ave Maria, Maria—"

"My dear, how terrible!" I exclaimed. "You don't agree with the radio and television reform. But let me remind you that we're now optimists and we're living in the New Era."

"David, my boy! How are you? Just fine I see; youthful and enjoying your job as Mr. President's pet child. Don't you like the song? I think it's of the New Era, although I'm not sure. How are things going? Have you seen the new cultural theater? We must go together. I believe that the most important auditorium will be inaugurated in a couple of weeks where a really gigantic show of propaganda called 'Experience of the New Era' will be performed."

"Yes, Eduardo told me. This show relates our national history from the arrival of the first native to Panama; it goes on with the native culture, the arrival of the Spaniards, of the Negro slaves, the independence, etc. the main part of the show is centered around the accomplishments of the new government, the programs to exterminate illiteracy and unemployment, poverty and hatred. It shows the family reform, the child raising and the labor programs and also the calender reform. All this with the help of films projected simultaneously, of slides, lighting and sound effects, and a great deal of really fantastic special effects that the best Hollywood producer could envy. I think Eduardo based it on a show called 'London experience' playing in London, although he improved the technique and elaborated the programming in order to propagate our social and psychological revolution. Of course, Eduardo says that it doesn't have anything to do with 'London Experience' and besides his show isn't propaganda for anyone or anything but is purely a presentation of the events of the New Era."

"How innocent, don't you think? I want to see this 'Experience of the New Era.'"

"Sure. There are now so many foreign visitors in the country who want one to take them to see everything, the clinics, the schools, the peasant communes, the substitute mothers' schools, the people meditating during the last five days of the year.... This has become hard work, Mercedes. I waste a lot of time playing tourist guide, since we've become important figures, and the revolution is mentioned throughout the world. Not too long ago, *Time Magazine* interviewed Mr. President and took photographs of many things; I hope the article turns out well, without too many changes or interpretations: after all, *Time* is a serious magazine. Martin was beaming when he told me that such an eminent publication had interviewed him, but I swallowed hard thinking of his messianic and grandiloquent exclamations which the North-American journalists surely don't understand and besides it doesn't suit their style. Anyway, today the New Era is talked about with certain respect although we have more enemies than friends. Popularity has brought a lot of people to Panama, but now that we have the 'Experience,' of Eduardo, I mean of the New Era, we can send the visitors to see it instead of taking them around ourselves."

Factual information was a very serious and difficult problem of the social communication reform. The international news agencies sent their cables to Panama just as always, bringing news of the United States President's trips, of the conflicts between the Arabs and the Jews in the Middle East, of earthquakes in Japan, of one or another scientific achievement from time to time. I was more in favor of our newspapers, radio and television transmitting everything in a candid and immediate way. The Commission did not agree, and each element of information had to be evaluated before it could be broadcast. This seemed dangerous to me, but after all, according to the communications experts, the "wrong information" was more dangerous. I had always thought that the more information the better.

I received journals on psychology and magazines of general

interest from abroad. I had not travelled for a long time, since the years I had dedicated to the new government did not allow me to move around. I had to be on top of so many things that the outside world lost its importance. Nevertheless even when I read the foreign journals through superficially, I was more and more convinced of the need to be informed, to know what was going on. This is a psychological necessity, just like eating, being healthy; right we should respect. The right to information, to the freedom of press. No one should cut off information, nor "purify" it; in this, the new government was wrong, and for the first time I disagreed with Mr. President and his collaborators.

CHAPTER 10
EDUCATION

The educational system of the New Era was a combination of personalized instruction, educational technology and long-term planning, with an emphasis on educational environment and continuing education. The education of a new man started when a couple decided to have a child, continued through the pregnancy, the child's birth, infancy, kindergarten, formal education, training in professional abilities and skill's acquisition. It still went on through twelfth grade or high school, and continued through university, for those who wished to attend. It even went on beyond any forms of educational institution.

Education stressed objectives and the development of skills and abilities. It recognized the taxonomy of educational objectives that initially were associated with the name of Bloom, and the numerous additions and modifications which were added to that name. It was an education for life; an education for self-education. In addition to cognitive development, affective factors were also emphasized. A child should learn to develop his emotions and aptly express them; love as much as hate, and anger as much as fear. Negative emotions had to be expressed through constructive channels instead of being ignored or restrained.

The preschool educational system was especially important; the slogan "first the children" was taken very seriously. This new education was neither of books nor of theories. It was an education of the cognitive potential and, at the same time, of the emotions, of motor skills, of social abilities. One learned how to give and receive love, to be positive in relating to other humans, to accept people and be accepted by them.

Nothing was left to chance. We did not expect people to grow spontaneously and ripen like a fruit. Learning was emphasized in the sense of behavior patterns modification and making them more and more adaptive and complex. In a wide sense, learning was one of the pillars of the new society; not the learning of concepts and knowledge, but the modification of behavior, in order to achieve specific and concrete goals.

We did not assume that people knew how to do anything. Specific training was given for everything. We had carefully outlined informal learning by discovery directed to the community. They sought short term and concrete goals which were integrated within long term general goals.

"The formation of a new man in this New Era was the concern of education. What can be done to achieve a more integral education will produce important social effects," said the Educational Commission in a report.

This education for life encompassed children, young people, adults, and the elderly. In each case the human potential of each group was considered, and integrated programs were proposed. The concept of continuing education included various reforms: communication media, community public libraries, cinema, theater plays, and the annual meditation meetings. The experts on education insisted that nobody really was able to teach something to someone else; one should learn on his own. The goal in education was self-education.

Besides the informal and continuing education, we had relatively traditional systems of primary, secondary, and tertiary (university) education. Professional studies at a national level were made concerning the needs of the country in the science, technology, commerce and services areas, and in the intermediate professions and occupations. When we raised the standard of living of the population, the work market was left unbalanced with the appearance of a large segment arising out of the population that before had belonged to the rural lower classes. These people were given training, work, adequate housing, and became integrated into the advantages of the New Era, including information, recreation, health and educational opportunities.

All these changes were taking place at the same time and each Commission worked to achieve important reforms. The social balance seemed to totter each time such a change was executed but it would finally return to its homeostatic level.

Ecology, which I consider the most important science of our time, was highly respected. A child was taught to respect and love nature, to achieve a balance between what he consumes and what he produces, not to destroy the environment, not to pollute the world. He was made to understand that an ecological balance was vitally important for all of us, because we are all members of the great biological family. Since irreparable abuse had occurred during the last centuries, the balance has been considerably altered. Before man arrived on different parts of the earth, there were forests; when man moved on, he left behind deserts. This is what we wanted to prevent at all costs.

Education for peace, for love, for harmonious social relationships. Education for self-education. Education for self-development. Education of the emotions, of the intellect, of the body, of sexuality, of language. Education to express aggression, fear, and anger. Education to prevent the need to feel envy or vengeance. Education so that another war would never be initiated.

"Too beautiful to be true," was the reaction of a distinguished Spanish woman educator who was visiting the country along with a group of educational experts of various nationalities.

"Education has always needed to be improved but there are insurmountable barriers to confront. For example, illiteracy. How did you eradicate illiteracy?"

"Through massive campaigns. It really wasn't so difficult," I answered, "We all feared that this would be an insuperable obstacle but we've wiped out illiteracy ever since the social reform was implanted two years ago."

"I see. Well, then, why do you think you have succeeded in an area in which all other countries have failed?" the lady inquired rather spitefully.

"They've all failed? What about Cuba? They were able to do away with illiteracy in less time than we were, Madam—"

"Another thing," interrupted a priest, "What role do you give to religion? We've visited schools for surrogate mothers, educational centers for the mentally retarded, kindergartens, schools for gifted children, universities, and vocational schools, but we haven't seen a cross, a priest or a religious worker in these educational centers. What contribution does religion make to this social revolution?"

"Look. We aren't religious people. We respect religion if someone wishes to have one, but we don't encourage it. We believe that everyone has a right to follow his religion if he wishes, and there are religious services and worships in various religions. On the other hand, it's not true that priests and religious workers have nothing to do with education. There are many priests, nuns, and others working in kindergartens, in universities, in vocational schools. Since they don't use habits, you don't realize that they're priests. But in reality they are and they do a magnificent work. They have an enviable dedication and capacity for work."

"William James once said that you should try to find the 'moral equivalent to war,' interrupted one of the members of the Educational Commission who was with us. "It would be something that would cause man to make sacrifices for others, to withstand cold, heat, hunger, in order to achieve an objective: neither war nor a warlike triumph, but a more human and positive objective for which people would do what they normally do to win a war or what they do during war time. Well, then we're looking for the 'moral equivalent to religion.'"

"The 'moral equivalent to religion' . . . similar to the moral to war that William James spoke about. . . ."

"Maybe the building of the new society has fulfilled this important psychological function. At least it has helped to give enthusiasm and strength to millions of people. It has been a collective, social undertaking, and many people have devoted all their energy, time, knowledge and abilities to this enormous struggle of really building a new society, of initiating a New Era."

"And the rebels? Don't you have any rebels, people who are opposed to all this? I don't know. I don't know. There must be something wrong in this. There are things that I don't understand and don't agree with. I know there are mistakes and that your New Era is going to collapse."

"For example, you have legalized sexual promiscuity and homosexualism. Although you are persistently against the consumption of alcohol, you encourage the use of marijuana."

"We don't encourage it," I explained. "Marijuana was legalized in reduced and controlled quantities. Its use is legalized, but its production and sale is a government monopoly, as are alcoholic drinks in many countries. Now, sexual reforms are a different story. They are included within the family reform, which we respect and encourage. The family is the basic cell of society and—"

"Including the homosexual family?"

This subject was not easy to deal with among a group of foreigners with prejudices and aversion toward our social reforms.

"We've legalized adult homosexuality by mutual consent; we've done the same with other sexual minorities. The law is similar to the one that exists in Holland or in Denmark; it's neither better nor worse. To this we've added contractual relationships, similar to marriage, with possibilities of adopting children and leaving a will. Homosexual marriages are something that have been discussed ever since the Greek era. There's nothing scandalous about it. What we've really done is legalize a situation and rationally solve a problem."

"Disgusting, simply disgusting!" exclaimed the Spanish lady, grabbing her husband's arm.

"It may be. Anyway, worldwide reaction has been most favourable. We've even received positive commentaries from various Catholic groups, including one from the United States called 'Dignity' that has fought for sexual dignity in all aspects. Many countries have proposed to their legislatures these contractual situations, meaning homosexual marriages, following the model that we've approved here."

"Strange, very strange. The Latin American machos boasting in defense of homosexual minorities. . . . And in a country like this one, in the middle of the tropics, full of pretty women."

"We don't *encourage* homosexuality just as we don't encourage the consumption of marijuana. We give very serious and responsible sexual education, adapted to the level of intellectual development of the person being educated. We also educate the community about sexual minorities. We don't want this kind of behavior to spread; we just want it to stop being a stigma and a cause for depression and disturbance for many people. We accept that each one loves *in his own way* without bothering others. We punish all sexual acts (hetero or homosexual) with under-age children, as well as physically or psychologically forced acts. We're against propaganda and leading people astray. This seems terrible to us."

"The Church in our country has approved this social reform, as well as other ones," explained one of my collaborators. "Curiously enough, there are more homosexual marriages between women than between men. In other words, more lesbians have thought it convenient to get married, according to the new laws of the country, than the male homosexuals."

"My God, how strange! It's so hot here. Could we leave now?" asked the Spanish lady.

CHAPTER 11
FAMILY AND SEXUALITY

In giving so much importance to the formation of a new man or a new society, the New Era had to decide how to change the family, that sacred and steadfast structure, whose crises peaked during the last years. The extensive family, aunts and uncles, cousins and grandparents, that enormous network of interrelationships into which a person is born, lives and dies, had been substituted in the last decades of the twentieth century by the nuclear family of the father, the mother and the children. This nuclear family was threatened by the winds of modernization, as a result of the growth of communications, of industrialization, and of the innovative nature of man. The death of the family was prophesied several times by many outstanding people like Cooper. The family was agonizing, struggling helplessly; its foundations were criticized and its right to exist was questioned.

We all knew that if the family was going to survive, it had to be transformed. But was its survival worthwhile? I strongly believed that it was. This implied many structural changes, beginning with creating better opportunities for women, so that they could free themselves from the traditional ties from the economic and legal dependency on men, in order to go out into the real world and fight for a place in the sun. At the same time she was required to remain sweet and feminine, caring for her children and her husband, managing both roles faultlessly. The tension, the conflict, was too much for many women. Some chose to return to housekeeping and forget about work, university and success. They preferred to wash diapers and add a drop of honey to their husband's lives. Others neglected their home, rejected once and for all marriage and children, lived alone or jumped from lover to lover, without meaning or direction. Anyway, as a result of social changes and the family crisis, the situation for women was tremendously difficult to deal with.

We had to think seriously about this problem and try to find solutions. One alternative was the test-tube baby of Huxley's *Brave New World*. That had been done several times before in England and in the United States, much to the horror of the more traditional segments of society. Another possibility was not to contract any unions or any marriages. Another was to have men live in one community and women in another.

"None of these. The family has its place in our society," was the conclusion of the Family and Sexuality Commission. "The family has to be changed, not eliminated."

The first step was to separate sexuality from reproduction, and the care of the children from marriage. To make love was one thing; to have children was something very distinct. People could marry with no intention of having children. Exhaustive information on family planning was distributed, about contraceptives and sterility. Those who desired to have children were helped in all possible ways to have them. We thought of setting a maximum limit of two children per couple, making it illegal to have more than two.

"Ours isn't a punitive society," Mr. President reminded us. "People should live happily and do what they like. But they should be conditioned to *like what they ought to like*."

"Conditioned is the wrong word," observed Mercedes, "People should 'learn' what is good for themselves and for society and behave accordingly. Things should be natural and spontaneous for them, not imposed. They should lead to satisfactory consequences. This means that people are conditioned to do what they ought to do, but without pressure or punishment, through their own will and initiative. This conditioning should begin at the moment of conception and be accepted as something natural, satisfying and strengthening. Nothing should be forced. Behavior should come from within the organism, not be unchained through stimulus."

"What the Commission did about the family and sexuality seemed to me quite right," observed Eduardo. "It consulted people about what they wanted, made national surveys, interviewed men and women of all ages, and analyzed opinions relating to the family crisis. It sought advice from the best anthropologists and sociologists in the country and from abroad. Do you remember the woman who came from England to advise us about family problems? As a result of all the consultations and all the social, anthropological, psychological and economic studies, important inroads were discovered."

"Yes, but only in the long run will we see the effectiveness of the solutions," Mercedes noted. "Just like the changes in our ways of behaving, educating children, working and living, it will bear fruits over a long period of time. The same can be said about the family from this point of view. Whether we've made the right solutions or not is something that history will reveal."

In the family reform the concept of *the couple* was maintained and given primary importance. The family was a man and a woman. There could be children or not. As an alternative, however, the act of living alone was respected. The government gave all its help to those who wished to have children, including free time for the woman, a part-time job if she wanted to work, and technical help. The children could be raised by the mother or by substitute mothers. The child-raising and adoption centers were given the best of budgets, since the slogan "the children first" was something we all accepted as a very important life value. Many women decided to keep their children; others preferred to put them up for adoption, without anguish or tears, knowing very well what they were doing; others gave them to be raised by substitute mothers, without losing their guardianship.

The marriage relationship was maintained, in both its legal structure and its inheritance laws. The latter were going to remain a very short time. We had thought of eliminating inheritance once and for all, in such a way that no one was born rich or poor and that nobody would think of hoarding a fortune in order to leave it to his children. The government would inherit everything. Since this would have created a general disagreement among the people, we decided it was better not to put such a reform into immediate use and we abandoned it for a couple of years.

Couples lived together before getting married. Marriage experts advised them not only to have a sexual relationship but also to live together for a while. It is not the same to receive a boyfriend as a visitor or to make love with him, as it is to live together several months in the same house, fix meals, clean floors, sleep, go to work and share holidays.

Getting married was easy and people married very young. Since sexuality and reproduction were clearly separated, it was not accepted that by getting married you automatically had to have children. Overpopulation problems of the planet resulted in advising people to marry later and later. However, we did not believe that getting married and having children were synonymous. A young marriage had the great advantage of solving the big sexual problem for young people. A man of twenty and a woman of eighteen are in their highest period of sexual interest and activity. To postpone marriage for another ten years was to deprive them of the possibility of having a fuller and more satisfying sexual life.

In getting married a woman did not change her last name for her husband's; instead she kept her own. The married woman carried a distinct identification; but she did not use her husband's last name.

Just as marriages were easy, so were divorces. People got divorced by mutual consent, with no social or economic pressure for staying together. A woman did not have to stay with a husband she did not love for fear of loneliness or hunger. Children were well-protected by legislation, but the main economic responsibility in relationships came from the government, rather than the parents. Nevertheless, parents were responsible for several important psychological obligations.

In legalizing homosexual marriage, the previously made points related to both heterosexual and homosexual couples. The latter could only adopt a child of the opposite sex; lesbians could only adopt a boy, and male homosexuals a girl. Furthermore, the adoption centers made exhaustive studies on the mental health and stability of the homosexual couple before allowing them to adopt a child. There were really very few cases in which such couples adopted children or were allowed to do so.

Almost everyone married. Few people chose to live alone permanently. Our critics predicted that we were going to do away with marriage and that by fomenting marriage among young people and facilitating divorces, no one would get married and the family would deteriorate more than before. But to the contrary, the family seemed to become stronger and more stable. I think the emphasis we put on the couple as the basic unit of society was very healthy and appropriate.

Children and young people were given a thorough and serious sexual education. Sexuality ceased to be a mystery and we did not fill into promiscuity or perversion. The fact of legalizing adult homosexuality by mutual consent did not increase homosexuality, but it did reduce the number of suicides among that tormented segment of the human race.

"Because no one has sexual problems, a psychoanalyst wouldn't have a job here," said a foreign visitor one time.

That was not true either. Psychoanalysts now devoted themselves to other things and no longer worked on the sexuality of their patients. Often they could be found in the mental health clinics. Although because of the emphasis our society puts on science, and the little compatibility that exists between psychoanalysis and science, we did not visualize a very promising future for the psychoanalysts of the New Era.

We had clubs for single people where a man or woman could go alone to find a sex partner for the night, for the weekend, or for life. They were clubs similar to those in other countries, but the fact that they existed in the tropics made respectable people's hair stand on end.

Of course, what caused even greater scandal were the Sexual Health Centers that were created in the capital and later on in other cities. We planned them with great care and attention. They were somewhat like the "swinger clubs" of the United States or the Turkish baths of Europe. Here, any adult, man or woman, could enter and remain as long as he or she wished. He had his own personal room; he could take a bath, walk nude through the hallways and other rooms, rest, make love with whomever he pleased, drink, eat, and sleep. These were not really pleasure houses, although orgies were plentiful, as well as that which was called "reckless sex" in the terminology before the New Era. Obviously no one charged for his sexual services.

A person could go after work and make love with four or five different people. The sex partner could be named or remain anonymous, be young or old; be attractive or ugly. Everyone decided with whom he would go to bed. People did as they pleased in bed and, in psychoanalytic terminology, one could say that it touched on "perverse and polymorphous sexuality." There was nothing further from us than making an evaluation of such behaviors.

The problem in the Sexual Health Centers, as in other similar places, was venereal diseases. We had done all possible to eradicate them, but in our beautiful tropical country they flared up again, in spite of our efforts. Medicine was socialized; there was no charge for medical services or for medicine. Advertising was done in support of health, but nevertheless venereal diseases continued to appear. The people who repeatedly went to these Centers, where they could turn their most secret sexual fantasies into reality, said that there rarely existed the chance of catching a venereal disease. At least no one confessed that he had picked one up. The day will come in which such diseases will have disappeared from the world, or at least, from our world!

Since the Sexual Health Centers were a controversial issue widely discussed among visitors, I was against allowing foreigners into such Centers. After all, similar places already existed in most of the industrialized countries, but they had never taken the precautions we had to prevent venereal diseases. Besides, the business of the Sexual Health Centers was often reported in the most important periodicals of the world (and in others not so important like *Playboy*). I think the best idea was to establish such Centers but not to publicize them. Foreigners were dying to do a "field study" of such places.

The family did not desintegrate because a man or a woman could go to these Centers, spend an hour with three different nameless sex partners, and return home to the husband or wife they really loved. Marriage relationships became stronger instead of weaker.

Elderly people occupied an important position in the family reform. Their potentialities were utilized for the welfare of society and for their own benefit. Older people were important in the New Era. They were highly regarded, cared for, and hopefully spent a fulfilling and happy existence without stirring up the pangs of the past or suffering the imminent arrival of death.

CHAPTER 12
THE OLD PEOPLE

A youth-oriented society such as those found in Western cultures, has no place for older people. It is believed that a man finishes his life at age 65 when he retires from work. His world shrinks, he loses his friends, his sense of importance, his independence and his self-determination. Retirement accelerates death, and the last years of a human being's life become a heavy load for himself as well as those around him.

The reality of growing old and dying is an experience known only by human beings. Man is the only animal that is aware he has to die. All philosophies and religions consider old age and death to be a part of the human existential reality, but man looks on them with anguish and insecurity. We cannot accept that we are all going to grow old and die. We do not like to think, just now, that someday our turn will come.

Skinner said that for an individualistic society death was the worst misfortune. In his opinion, the survival of a culture is a very important value, and, apparently, to know that we have contributed to the human culture can be sufficient consolation for us, so that we do not fear death because afterwards our work lives on.

"Lies, lies," commented Martin. "Death is a terrible misfortune and we have done little more than invent excuses and silly consolations. Worst of all, it is inhuman and absurd to think that there's life after death. Science has demonstrated that beyond all doubt, the conscience, the individuality, depends on the brain. When it desintegrates we will be dead. There won't be any resurrection. There's no last judgment. Obviously, there's neither heaven nor hell."

"Hell is other people. It is the injustices, the anguish, the pain, the social diseases of our life," Mercedes noted.

"Yes, and one invents consolations from beyond the grave for lack of other alternatives. People invent a life after death to comfort themselves from an unjust and painful world. If only we could change the world to make it better here and now instead of inventing posthumous worlds," added Eduardo.

"That's what we're doing," pointed out Mr. President with his omnipotence and messianic spirit.

"The Skinnerian solution of death doesn't convince me either," I said. "It's only another consolation, similar to the Christians' paradise or the Hindu Nirvana."

The discussion went on and everyone aired his viewpoints. We talked about all we had done to benefit the elderly and about what we thought had to be done concerning death.

"Everyone should have the freedom *to choose* the day of his death, and his own way to die. Old age locked into illnesses has no human meaning. We'll have to give the elderly the possibility of living or dying with dignity and honor, through scientific means."

"But, Martin, that would be suicide."

"No, it would be euthanasia. Really, in my country much remains to be done. This issue of death is very important. For fear of worldwide criticism, I've never proposed that the Human Development Commission studies everything which is related to maturity and old age and death. They would say that in the New Era we're killing people, when in reality what we're doing is allowing them to choose the day of their death, to leave everything in order, instead of waiting until their machinery breaks down and death tricks them."

I imagined the day of my death. It should be preceded by various months of psychological as well as practical preparation. Everything should be in order. Possessions in the power of the children; professional activities in the hands of my successors. After a traditional-type therapy, a little Rogerian and a lot existential, I would say good-bye to my most immediate collaborators and send farewell letters to acquaintances. Just like that, without anguish or irrational fears. The world would keep on turning after my death. First, I would enter a special hall, and then I would go to a room with a chair or a bed in front of a large screen where beautiful, peaceful scenes would be projected. Gas would slowly fill the habitation and, without thinking much about it, suddenly death would overcome me.

Brrr! Although it may sound very rational, it really gave me chills to think of it. It gave me a crazy desire to jump up and say that I was still young and alive, and that according to statistics, I was not going to die for another 30 years.

"Before a person chooses his death, he should first have to fulfill several criteria," suggested Martin. "He should be over sixty years old. No one should need him, neither his children, nor his spouse, nor his professional associates. I believe a person has no right to die if people need him. It's not fair to abandon small children, sick parents, and people who would definitely be harmed by his death."

"I'm against suicide," I said. "As an optimistic man, I think problems have a solution and that nobody should take his own life."

"Except in conditions of old age and illness. In those cases, it's more compassionate to help someone to die than to force him to live against his will."

Curiously enough, and unlike what we were talking about in Panama, we had created an enormous Research Institute for the Prolongation of Life. It depended on an adequate budget and we had invited the principal world specialists to work there. We still did not know what would be the results of the investigations that were in process in this Institute. I always thought that we had founded it because of our tremendous fear of death. We harbored the childhood fantasy that thanks to the Institute's scientists, someday life would be prolonged. We would stand further and further from the spectre of death. Until finally we would not be able to maintain a distance and then. . . .

The programs for the elderly went along very well and generated worldwide interest. They encompassed economic, medical, psychological, laborial and recreational factors. The government gave more money to the managers than they would receive from their retirement pay, because the Human Development Commission found, much to everyone's surprise, that the elderly had many economic problems. The medical programs were easy to implement as were the psychological ones. It was necessary to incorporate intensive courses on geriatrics and on gerontological psychology for doctors and psychologists who were interested in the subject. At last we succeeded in having qualified personnel.

The labor program, however, was not easy to implement. According to our ideals, people needed to be useful, to do work that had meaning; therefore, it was necessary to find jobs for the elderly. That was easier for women than for men because we discovered that older women could fill positions in kindergartens better than younger ones.

The same results were found in various professional activities, services and other areas. We analyzed which aptitudes and interests were required for different jobs, in order to determine whether an elderly person could fill them in a useful way. As a result the older person would feel satisfaction and the job would be well done.

The recreational programs were not limited to sedentary or

artistic activities. In addition to playing the guitar, painting, and reciting poetry, the elderly were taking country excursions, and doing physical exercise. I even saw some who climbed small mountains. All this was directed and planned. In the New Era, nothing was left to chance except the moment of death—at least until Mr. President dared to propose his program of euthanaasia, and face the international storm that was going to befall him for daring to make such a proposal.

The older people were integrated into the work force and assimilated into the New Era. Just like children, they smiled as they walked along the streets with their peers, as well as with the young. They could be found wearing bright colors, having "modern" ideas and actively participating in community activities. On meditation days at the end of the year, the older people almost served as a memory bank to society to remind people what the world had been like before the beginning of the New Era. Older people were respected and loved. We treated them with affection. We never considered them a nuisance and they knew that they occupied a place of great importance in society.

All the programming positions were held by young people. Many were under thirty years old. We were young and revolutionary, full of energy, enemies of routine, and enthusiastic and fervent craftmen of social change. The oldest one of us was Mr. President, and his attitude of elsest brother was very noticeable. This government of young men loved children and old people. It respected science; did not interfere with philosophical and religious beliefs of others and wanted everyone to be happy and productive. The only difference was that we planned everything with great care and wanted people to be "conditioned" (pardon, to "learn") to behave themselves as they should.

"Everyone is happy now. But if some groups are happier than others, I think they are children and the elderly."

CHAPTER 13
MARIBEL

The New Era had begun four years ago. The group of North American advisors, which we familiarly called the Group of Ten, had been with us for two years and then departed. During that time, I had worked a great deal, without rest, workdays of ten to twelve hours, including F days. During vacations I had moved to other Panamanian towns to go on working. My work as a psychologist had weakened a great deal. I hardly studied and I think, little by little, I lost interest in making a name for myself as a researcher. Collaborating with the government for four years was enough. Mr. President needed me to work day and night, to train people, to write programs, to meet with the individual commissions. I was happy doing this. It was ecstasy but also agony. Sometimes I ran out of strength; I felt really "burnt out" like an old fuse.

I was almost thirty-five. My God, half of my life, since I would probably live 70 years, in spite of stubborn investigations that were taking place in the Research Institute for the Prolongation of Life. I had done a lot in my years, but I still felt I could have done much more.

The F day began cloudy and dismal. The night before we had worked late in the office with Eduardo and Mercedes. I had promised myself to rest all day. I had not done that for a long time. Even on the meditation days at the end of the year, I dedicated my time to teaching others how to think over their pasts, evaluate their achievements and plan their future. From training others to do this, I forgot to do it myself.

I woke up tired. It was two o'clock and the sun shone in all its splendor. I turned over in bed and tried to go back to sleep. Unable to, I got up, washed, shaved and listened to the news of the day. I felt dull, almost sick, although the doctors had told me that I was in excellent shape in spite of my long working hours, the stress, the responsibility, and the difficult position I occupied as the dictator's reliable man and planner of this whole gigantic social experiment.

If I had followed my natural impulses, I would have shouted:
"Finally the eternal weariness has come
to rest before my eyes;
the weariness of the dying day
and of the coming dawn."

Since it was not good to let oneself be taken by these periodical depressions which we tried to avoid in our people, I decided to hold my head up and do something I had never done before. I decided to go to one of the Sexual Health Centers. I went to one far from my house, in other words, one that operated on F day (it was F day only in some city zones).

An hour later I was in my small room, talking with a girl somewhere between twenty and twenty-five. She was a slender blonde, rather pretty and uncomplicated, a woman of few words.

"What is your name?"

"Maribel. And yours?"

"David. I have an important position, you know. That's why I prefer not to tell you the whole name. No, it doesn't matter, you're a good girl. My name is David González," I bragged.

She smiled a foolish grin. I had expected that she would shout that it was incredible. That she felt proud to know me. That she was going to tell all her girlfriends from the university or from work that she had met me. Instead of saying all that, she smiled like an absolute idiot.

"What do you do?" she asked me.

I felt like dying, or better yet, that she should die, just like that, without planning it, without help from science. Dead at 20, in a Sexual Health Center.

"Lady, if you ask that, then it means that you never read the papers," I said pretentiously. "I'm the main advisor to Mr. President and everyday there's something in the newspapers about what we're doing. At least there's something in the *Official Journal* which is printed in the National Palace."

"No, I don't read the newspapers, they're quite boring. If you have any influence in the government, I suggest that you think about changing a few things. For example, the advertisements along the streets or the songs on the radio. They are very serious and boring, you know."

"Serious and boring?"

"Yes, love. A girlfriend of mine who studies sociology made a list of the principal advertisements and found out that they offer very few ideas and concepts. The ads everywhere say such things as 'peace and love,' 'let's build a world,' 'life is where the people are,' 'no more war,' 'children first,' 'don't leave anything to fate.' They're boring ideas. People read them a thousand times a day: on the bus, train, billboards, posters. They hear them on the radio and see them on television. We're full of it. Always the same thing, ten times an hour. How boring, love!"

"Maybe so, lady. However, our revolution is quite permissive and liberal, not like the revolutions of other countries—China or Cuba for example. We're in favor of sexual freedom and we don't oppose alcohol or marijuana in reasonable, carefully controlled quantities."

"God, spare me from the Chinese, the Russians and the North Americans."

"We respect God, you see," I said with enthusiasm. "We don't allow anti-religious advertising, but we don't permit religious proselytizing either. The government's advertising is the only one allowed, and it is focused on proverbs like the ones you're seen: 'no more war,' 'children first,' etc. What's wrong with that? We want to educate the people and that's what we're doing."

"Even though you're all young, you're quite serious. Remember, love, people don't care about ideology or philosophy. All they want is to be left alone to live in peace, to have a stable job, education, health, and a few vacations on the beach each year."

"I always wondered if the future wouldn't be like a Middle Age instead of a Renaissance. It's not possible that humanity continues progressing so much, discovering so many things, inventing, polluting the atmosphere, making war—"

"Instead of making love," she said.

"Yes, that's it. People today don't want to worry about anything. They think that there's nothing worth losing sleep over, nothing that creates anguish or desperation. We haven't found the moral equivalent to war. Our children are mediocre, they only search for immediate satisfactions. Yes, now I believe it. We're headed toward a Middle Age, stability and mediocrity, where no one will progress or suffer. Look, my dear. Do you think there's someone who wants to become an Einstein or a Beethoven? Tell me. You, yourself. Would you like to become a Marie Curie?"

Her eyes sparkled when hearing this, but she did not say anything. No, without a doubt, this skinny girl, lying nude next to me had absolutely no interest on becoming a Marie Curie.

"That Middle age will soon be here. No more discoveries, no more inventions, no more worries or ideological confrontations. Everything will be planned, everyone will be happy. All will be explained. People will enjoy life and have plenty of peace, and time will go by, empty and meaningless. This Middle Age, unfortunately, will be the consequence of our beautiful social and psychological revolution. How absurd, how absurd! We will have planned the society and the environment, have *programmed* and *conditioned* man, using today's most efficient scientific methods. The result won't be human-robots, as our enemies from the United States and Russia say, but happy and mediocre people like you."

"Bad, baby. Although I really don't know if it will be so bad. After all, it's the goal sought by humanity. A society without hunger, without illiteracy, without physical or mental illnesses, without Beethovens or Einsteins. Of course we could program man to have more or less existential anguish, to become more rebellious or more obedient. Behavior modification works the same in one way as in another. What we've done is change man to become peaceful, good and mediocre. We could make him readier for his environment, full of existential anguish, in such a way that he would become an Alexander the Great, or Sartre."

"Thank you very much. Don't you do it, David. Leave us alone. To be happy and peaceful, there's nothing wrong with that. Maybe something won't function right with one or another of your children who are conditioned and programmed to be good and happy. That child will be the genius that you are looking for, the Alexander the Great who will conquer the world. Hopefully, his presence will be delayed, and the conditioning programs will be so perfect that such anguished geniuses will *never* appear to agonize the rest of us mortals."

"The Middle Age will give way to another Renaissance, and later to another period of creativity and unrest such as the Modern Age; and later there will be another Middle Age, just like the one we're about to start."

"Everything's a big circle, love."

"Yes, Maribel. It's the infinite return of Nietzsche."

"Lie down, love. I think people like you weren't born to live in the New Era, in you beautiful Middle Age where no one suffers problems or existential anguishes. You were born to change the world, to build the New Era but not to enjoy it. You and your people, those on top, those who have offices in the Presidential Palace, weren't born to live as the common herd, happy and good, in the New Era. Something went wrong in your early conditioning, love."

CHAPTER 14
THE ARMY AND THE POLICE

I was sorry never to see Maribel again. I remember that she left the room, climbed the carpeted stairs and turned into the television room. I assumed that from there she would go to the pool, the sauna or the orgy parlor. What was certain was that she disappeared from my sight—and from my life—although I would have liked very much to see her again.

One day we had to talk over the very important national military and police forces. During the first years we had maintained the police as a control measure, but with the hope of one day being able to eliminate it from the country. The army performed the same function, outside the country. Military and police corps really belonged to the past, and I would have liked to quickly dissolve them. Since it was not easy to control people born before the New Era through positive reinforcement practices, the police had to be maintained.

"The more internal control that exists, the less external control that is required," our expert on adversive conditioning explained to us. "Society relies a lot on punishment and on aversive consequences as a temporary effect, unless we apply high intensity stimuli."

"Punishment on a social level must be eliminated," said Martin. "We've eliminated it on an individual level: no one punishes his children, and look what cheerful and beautiful children we have in Panama. They're healthy and happy, truly free and creative."

Remembering my conversation with Maribel the day before, I swallowed in silence.

"The aversive contingencies have to be eliminated sooner or later," continued our expert on punishment, avoidance and escape. "It's urgent to decide if the internal control is sufficient so this can be executed immediately. Four years have passed and we still have the army and the police. We have jails, violation fines—"

"But we also have rewards for those who respect the law," interrupted Mr. President, who day by day demonstrated less patience. "We have *positive reinforcements,* programmed gratifying consequences in all environments and adaptive behaviors."

"Yes, Sir. But supposedly the police are keeping order in many human activities, since we have to deal with people born before the New Era."

"Like ourselves" I noted.

"Yes, Sir. Like all of us. To do away with the army and the police depends on whether the people are sufficiently conditioned to be able to function without such discriminatory stimulus and aversive consequences. Let me explain. A person must have 'absorbed' law and order so that we can eliminate the police. The control should be internal and not external. Once the police are *inside* him, they have no reason to exist outside too."

Hours passed before the discussion finished. We concluded that we had to wait for a longer time; our revolution still had not sufficiently developed in order to completely eliminate the police.

The situation with the army was different. I urged that we terminate this organization. If someday we are at war with our enemies, the United States, USSR, or China, we really won't need an army, because we will have lost the war from the very beginning anyway. Obviously we cannot compete with such giants. On the other hand, we do not have any more enemies. Our army would only exist from waging war on neighboring countries, and this was against our philosophy of brotherly love and universal harmony.

"To have an army implies that we're ready to defend ourselves or to attack; that we believe in punishment, in weapons," I noted. "We've filled the people's minds with such phrases as 'no more war,' and we still have an army ready for war. With whom? We don't have any enemies. The strong political powers, such as the United States, Russia and China, who look unfavorably on what we're doing here, have so much power that it would be foolish to pit ourselves against them even if we wanted to. Besides, we don't want to. To have several thousand men in an army, ready to start war with another Third World country is something contrary to our philosophy. We're never going to initiate any war. And if we have no army, no one is going to attack us. There are small countries, like ours, without armies, which arouse worldwide sympathy and free them from attack by their neighbors. These countries exist in Africa and in Latin America. The rest of the countries are armed to the teeth, as we are."

My arguments were taken seriously, which surprised and amazed me. We were going to abolish the army, and keep the police to maintain social control until our programs were sufficiently understood in order to make their existence unnecessary. One day we would be a people without an army or police. A country that loved peace and demonstrated it before the eyes of the world.

Once we had no army, many countries that had looked upon us with certain distrust began to see us favourably. It was proof that we had pacifist intentions; that we were not satisfied with empty words. We believed in *reward,* not punishment. We believed in *peace,* not in war. All the projects on close human relationships, of bettering human life became more genuine now that we had eliminated the major force of aversive control. The "moral conscience" of the society ceased to be external and became *internal*.

Moreover, in the course of a year's time, we considered eliminating the police. Meanwhile we would restructure the moral education programs in the sense of Kohlberg and his sixth phase of moral maturity. The people who have reached this sixth phase agree with the society's system of rules in order to avoid social chaos; it's the highest level of moral development and all of our people should attain it. The preceding phases involve the following of norms to avoid punishment and accept authority; a person thinks of his own well-being or the well-being of others. The sixth phase was the goal, the social well-being, considering humanity as our object and not as a reduced segment of the same.

"Proceed in such a way that your actions establish a universal principle," quoted Mercedes from Kant. "It's the categorical imperative. Proceed in such a way that your actions establish a universal principle. Will we ever get to that point?"

"I think so. There's a lot that can be done in the area of moral development, but it has almost never been attempted. We have to condition people to want to do what's right so that they enjoy doing it. We're not going to obey a law for fear of punishment, but because we've internalized the positive reinforcement which results from doing what's right. Obviously we define 'right' in a humanistic context: 'right' is what's right for man, not what follows platonic canon laws of righteousness that don't belong to this world."

"Differing from religious consolations, our society, our 'kingdom,' is part of this world and not of another."

We continued to discuss morals and ethics, cultural relativism, what is right and what is wrong, which only can be improved when looking at humanity as a whole, as a conceptual framework, something that unites us rather than separates us. Norms should exist inside man thanks to a profound program of moral conditioning. In this way the police becomes unnecessary and each one of us is his own guardian of social and moral order.

"Today I was visited by a group of young people who proposed the legalization of many illegal chemical substances, especially hallucinagenic drugs. I've always been against these, you know, I believe a person should find his 'kicks,' his 'ecstasy,' through nature, work, love, or sports, but not through drugs."

"Yes, Dave," observed Mercedes, "By legalizing marijuana and turning its cultivation, processing, and distribution into a government monopoly, we've opened the door to the expectations of these groups of youngsters. We make vigorous campaigns against drugs, we dedicate a lot of time and money to fight against their use. In this aspect we're quite a puritanical society, much more puritanical than most countries. We believe that drugs decay a man's mind, destroy his individualilty and his personality."

"But, at the same time, we've legalized marijuana."

"That is, we've put it in another category. We don't consider it a 'drug,' or a forbidden substance. Its use is permitted under controlled conditions, in reduced quantities and after knowing in detail its primary and secondary side effects, its dangers and possible complications."

"We think alcohol is more dangerous than marijuana."

"It is. But since people have become accustomed to think of marijuana as something prohibited, now that it's been legalized, they ask us to do the same with heroine, cocaine, LSD and other crap. That's why it was risky to legalize marijuana."

"The preliminary studies we made didn't show that people would go from marijuana to 'stronger' drugs. This was an idea that everyone shared, but controlled studies affirmed the contrary. We legalized marijuana knowing well its effects. And for this same reason, we doubled our efforts against morphine, cocaine, heroin, LSD and other drugs."

Among other things, we had needed the police to fight against the drug traffic, but it had diminished considerbly; in the New Era people did not smoke much, did not drink much (except Mr.

President) or consume much marijuana either. Nevertheless, once the police were eliminated, how were we going to handle this problem?

The centers for drug addicts had all the services of detoxification, medical and psychological therapy, social assistance, and community education. The Narcotics Anonymous, similar to Alcoholics Anonymous, was doing marvelous work in this aspect and, by taking marijuana off the "black list," off the "index" of forbidden substances (as the Catholic Church had its "index" of forbidden books), many myths were broken. For the most part, the problem had been solved. Now, fewer drugs were consumed than before and there was a greater social conscience and sense of responsibility.

"I, who have never in my life smoked marijuana," I said, "feel strange when I explain to a group of parents why we've legalized it. They must think that my arguments result from a personal interest, but they're wrong. You know, it's the beginning of 'cognitive disonance' of Festinger."

"Something that we behaviorists don't believe in, Dave!"

"No? Ah, you're right, Mercedes. We don't believe in that. But it seems to work, at least a little. People think that I approve of legallizing marijuana because I'm a hard-core consumer of grass. On the contrary, if I were, I wouldn't be worried about the problem. But I'm not, I've never tried it nor do I think of trying it. It produces a state of 'cognitive dissonance' which has to be eliminated."

"It's curious how the human mind works."

"The 'mind' Mercedes? That's another structure that we behaviorists don't believe in either."

CHAPTER 15
THE NEW FAMILY STRUCTURE

Eliminating the army affected no one. The enormous human potential of that institution became a part of the productive social activities of the country. The budget for maintaining a group of persons highly qualified in the art of killing was passed on to other sectors of National Planning. I had always wondered why so many young, intelligent, disciplined persons were confined in military barracks waiting for a war that would never happen. In the army, they had scientific investigation, intelligence, enormous resources of human potential. Why did the United States want so many experimental psychologists in the army? There were people who specialized in perception, learning, cognitive psychology, experimental social psychology, in addition to mountains of engineers, doctors, physicists and chemists. Without a doubt, the "national defense" needed help from science and this seemed quite certain.

For us, an obscure country within the world panorama, a country without any international importance, the army represented only a method of defending ourselves from any attacking neighboring countries. It helped us to have 'status' and to feel strong. To do away with the army implied that we believed in peace and human brotherhood.

Contrary to the pessimistic predictions, the military men became easily integrated into the national productive forces. Several of them occupied governmental positions, including positions of relative responsibility. Since Mr. President had been in the army, he maintained profound friendships with many military men. And although "influences and contacts," so characteristic of Latin America, played no role in the New Era, it was nevertheless necessary to give ex-military men important positions.

In the past the army had led Mr. President to power. Today things were quite different. The process of social change had progressed considerably; Martin did not maintain his position through military force. We all worried about what could happen with this question of military support for Mr. President. But since the military men were happy in their new jobs, life went on as usual with no traces of a "coup d'état" or a 'counterrevolution," as we had feared. The new regime was definitely solidified, and the social and psychological revolution had already bore many fruits.

The ex-military men became an important productive power which had to be trained, but a to a reduced expense. Their discipline, order, and work capacity were easily used in the new society.

One night I was thinking of all this when I heard someone knock at my door. It was my friend Mercedes. She had a ten-year-old boy who was the son of a military, ex-husband of Mercedes, one of those who had been assimilated into society. In his case it was easy because he was a mining engineer, with adequate training and a great deal of experience. The boy, Felipe, was very intelligent, just like his mother.

"David, may I ask you a favor?" said Mercedes, entering my apartment. "I have a lot to do and I would like you to take care of Felipe. I have to go out, it's something urgent. I wondered if you could watch him for a couple of hours?

"Of course. I'll be glad to take care of Felipe. Hello, kiddo! How are you? I see you've grown a lot and soon you'll have a big deep voice like your father, and a moustache to charm the girls. Come here, son. I'm sure we'll have a good time. I was just about to sit down and read. I have finished dinner so I have nothing important to do."

"Thanks, Dave. What were you going to read?"

"A German study on family changes. Our changes have been more revolutionary than any other previous experiments. For example, the training of substitute mothers, the emphasis on young marriages, the separation of sexuality and reproduction, the rational family planning, the ease to marriage and divorce, the importance devoted to the children and the elderly. I want to see how much importance they give in Germany to the changes in the family structure that we've achieved here."

"Interesting. I'm sure you can read it when I get back. Goodbye, darling. I'll see you later. Bye, Felipe, be good. Don't torment your Uncle David too much. Since he has no children he doesn't know about the delights of living with a little monster, I mean, angel, like you."

"Good-bye Mercedes. I'll take care of Felipe and I'm sure we'll enjoy each other."

Mercedes left and I put aside my magazine for the tenth time in several days. I never had time to read anything of interest to me which was not part of my immediate job. I wondered what Felipe and I could do to spend a couple of hours together.

"Are you interested in family changes, Uncle David?" said Felipe who always called me Uncle. "Look. I have a couple of friends whose fathers stays at home to clean and cook, while their mothers go to work. Other friends are raised by mothers, some of them are unmarried, others are divorced. Other friends are raised by fathers who are divorced or widowed. Let's go visit some of them.

It'll be fun. In most cases the other children at school make fun of the classmates with no fathers or mothers, with unordinary families or who have been adopted by unmarried women."

Gustavo, Felipe's friend, lived close to my apartment. We went over and Felipe walked in as if he were at home. We sat on the floor in the playroom of Gustavo and his brothers and sister, and waited for the father who was in the kitchen washing the dinner dishes.

"Good evening," said Gustavo's father, entering the children's playroom. "Welcome, don't get up. Forgive me for not having greeted you before, but with three children to take care of, things are quite difficult. How are you, Felipe? It's been a long time since I've seen your father. Tell him I said hello. I guess he's adapted to his new life as a government engineer instead of a military engineer. It seems the army's assimilation into productive society only involved a change of titles and nothing else. Ah, but one thing's for sure, the ex-military men have to work more than before! I don't imagine there was any great problem for their social adaptation."

"Good evening. Felipe asked me to come with him to visit his little friends. It's nice to be here. You have three children?"

"Yes, Sir. Three adopted children. I'm unmarried and I've adopted three children, something that would have been impossible before the New Era. I work all day at home, in a government job of Social Communication. I analyze people's complaints and protests that are published in newspapers and magazines, or on the TV or radio, etc. I'm something like an analyst of the contents of mass media. In this way I have my office in the house and I'm here most of the time. The children go to school and come home to eat, play and whatever. I take charge of everything: preparing the meals, arranging their clothes, helping them with homework and giving them emotional support. You know, lately, a great deal of importance is given to matters of psychological nature."

"He's an unmarried father, Uncle David."

"I see. And why don't you get married?"

"For many complicated reasons. Besides, they're part of my private life. I prefer not to share them, at least not now. The children are very important to me and in deciding not to marry I anticipated a lonely life. Fortunately the new law enables unmarried men and women to adopt children, which I did. I have two boys and a girl, and I consider myself an ideal father. I know very well that the possibility of having my job at home helped a lot."

"I see."

"You know, I'm not that unusual. There are many unmarried mothers and unmarried fathers like me. More frequently you find women who want to have a child without getting married or who find no one with whom to have a child. This latter is less common because since marriage has been simplified and made more practical and functional today, everyone meets someone to marry if he wants to. Do you want some statistics? Because of my work, I'm familiar with many."

"My uncle is too," interrupted Felipe. "He and my mother have very important and responsible positions in the government. At least that's what they alway say. That's the reason why they never have time to take me to the movies."

"Sure, dear. Look. According to the statistics, twenty-two percent of the children grow up in homes with only one of their parents, usually the mother. As far as I know, in the United States it's seventeen percent. In other words, there's not much difference. Most of these homes with just one parent are managed by the women.

"They're divorced women," continued Gustavo's father, "or women who just decide to have one or several children, with the explicit intention of raising them by themselves. About three percent are homes with a father and no mother, due to divorce or death of the woman, or to the adoption of the children by an unmarried man. According to statistics there is an increase in this tendency, and I think that in ten years fifty percent of the children born today will live in a home with just one parent. The substitute mothers are wonderful. They're quite practical and perform a magnificent social service. Very admirable! Their work with abandoned children has been fantastic. The phrase 'the children first,' which is one of the pillars of the New Era, has enormously benefited the children."

"Aren't there any substitute fathers?" asked Felipe.

"No, dear. Our society still hasn't thought about it. What a mistake, no? I'll tell my boss in Social Communication to mention it to the directors of the Commission on Family and Sexuality. We've trained substitute mothers, whom I use every once in a while for my three children, but not substitute fathers. A child needs a masculine identification figure as well as a feminine one, and for heaven's sake, we've forgotten about this. I'll jot it down in my notebook to call my boss tomorrow and ask him to mention it at the next National Planning meeting."

"I hardly know any child who is being raised by both parents," said Gustavo. "At school they teach me that in every family there are a father, a mother, children, one or more maids, aunts and grandparents. I've never found this. Most of my friends have mothers and no fathers; I've a father and no mother. There are never any maids. Definitely, this is very strange, Dad."

"But we're all happy now," I observed defensively. "And in the New Era children come before anything else."

"The family is changing a lot and it's for the better. I feel that these reforms represent considerable progress, something that really no other country has dared to try before. Something that will be talked about during the coming centuries."

Positively or negatively? I asked myself. I think that it will be postively.

"The children who grow up in adoption centers are very happy," said Felipe. "Some of my best friends live in adoption centers, and they usually get the best grades, are the best football players and know more jokes and stories than the other kids."

"I think," I said very seriously, "that the difference between our society and other attempts of making a utopian society, lies in the use of scientific psychology. We're the first who have attempted to make a better society based on psychology and that's why we've come so far. Psychology was never been taken seriously until we, I mean our country, made maximum use of it. Now, look at all we've achieved. The potential of scientific psychology for human and social well-being is truly unlimited."

"I guess you're right, although that's not my area. Therefore I can't give an informed opinion on the matter. Anyway, we've worked a lot with the family and with the children. I was surprised to read in the newspaper a couple of days ago that there really exists no convincing evidence to support the belief that parental love during infancy protects the child from posterior pathology. In other words, much remains to be done in the area of early childhood experience. The big problems still exist."

"Do you think so? We've advanced a lot. A couple of centuries ago children were punished until they bled so that they would learn the alphabet. They obeyed older people, and were submissive and docile. They were socialized always through aversive practices. The further back one goes, the worse the treatment of children. Today things have changed for the better. Children aren't physically punished anymore; they aren't made to drink a quart of urine to learn to control enurisis, so that they don't wet the bed. This occurred in the seventeenth century. Children were separated from their parents for years in remote boarding schools, and this is not done anymore. We've progressed considerbly. The whole world has advanced. We've done a lot, but even so, it's the entire civilization that has progressed with regard to respect for children and their well-being."

After the conversation was over, I said it was time to take Felipe back to his mother. So we left. I think it was an interesting talk and I appreciated having exchanged ideas with one of the "consumers" of the family reform that we had planned and carried out "from above," from the government palace.

"I'd like to have a little boy like you," I told Felipe as we walked towards Mercedes' house. "A beautiful and intelligent child like you."

"Why don't you have one, Uncle? They showed me in the sexual education class how it's done. It seems to me quite easy. All you have to do is—"

"Yes, yes. I already know. But I would have to work less in order to spend time with my son, so that the reforms we try to instill won't be only theoretical, since 'charity begins at home.'"

"Does that seem so terrible for you? I think deep down inside it's fun. And you would enjoy it very much. Besides, I think that you wold do it very well."

CHAPTER 16
SCHOOL AND SOCIETY

I kept up my friendship with Felipe, Mercedes's son, who called me "Uncle" because of my friendship with his mother. We went out a lot, visited his little friends' families, schools, and training centers for substitutte mothers. A child teaches a grown up person how to see the world in a new dimension, takes him back to his own childhood. But childhood was not the same. Now there are fewer frustrations, less bitterness, less anger. Children are healthier and happier. They feel less guilt. There are fewer cases of parents who mistreat and take advantage of their children, fewer cases of suicide among children, less hate and envy. We had hoped that soon such negative emotions would disappear forever. Children no longer run away from home as they did in my time. Felipe and his little friends had not been born within the New Era, which had begun only four years ago, so without a doubt they still showed traces of the old system. But the day will come when everything will be new and better, when the last person who saw the Old Era finally dies, when all of us finally die.

One afternoon Felipe and I were at his school. I was interested in seeing how one of these institutions operated; not as a guide to answer questions, but as a visitor with some questions to ask myself. It was more fun. You could risk anything you wanted, and for me this was a rest compared to my role in National Planning, proposing solutions and giving answers to so many things.

Felipe's school was spacious and full of gardens. It was located on the outskirts of the city and resembled more a vacation farm than a school. In a way it was like Skinner's *Walden Two*. But it also resembled a Soviet pioneer camp. When I asked the teacher replied:

"The most important likeness refers to the influence of the children in the management of the school, in decision making, and in maintaining discipline. Here, just like Soviet education, we have children's councils that evaluate the others, give them rewards and impose punishments. Never physical punishment, of course, but more than anything, punishments through response cost programs. With the teachers and directors they discuss school plans, organize curricular and extracurricular activities, for example, excursions to the mountains to observe animals or sports competitions. They also control discipline.

"I would like to see it put into practice. Would that be possible?"

"Yes, but a bit later. There's a fifth-grade children's council in session right now. However, I don't think we can go until a little later."

"And what about formal education? And content teaching?"

"Here, we emphasize self and integral development of the individual, their behavior patterns, their feelings, as well as their formal knowledge. For the latter we depend on educational technology: films, the so-called teaching devices and so on. In most cases in the school we build the audiovisual aids, the aquariums, the terrariums, the coin and map collections. We do everything that can be done here. Films, educational units and other things difficult to produce locally, are given to us by the government."

"This school seems wealthy and prosperous."

"All of them are. There are big classrooms and gardens, a lot of space. The child is ouside much of the time. We emphasize integral education, and the language education of interpersonal relationships, of emotional behavior. It's important that the child socializes, we even prefer to say that he humanizes. The school is a part of the family, the community, and the working world. Parents often come here and we go to their homes. We want the children to participate actively in the adult's lives, to learn the roles that they will assume later, to become integrated into the working world."

"It's been said that in contemporary society children are absolutely useles."

"That's the way it was before. The school was one of the main alienating elements of man. Today it's different. As one famous educator said, 'schools were fortresses of cleanliness, order and boredom.' Today they're not as clean or orderly, and definitely they're not boring."

"I'm sure they're not. But formal education is quite rigid and systematic, isn't it? I believe learning is often done through modules, in which subjects become integrated. This helps to avoid lack of attention and of understanding."

"Yes. The modules work well. We have clear and specific objectives, and programmed subjects that are taught according to the previous learning level. School curricula are structured on learning units which are organized in hierarchies."

"And the influence of other children?"

"Subjects are preprogrammed in educational packages. But no one is taught anything without a previous explanation of the reasons why it has to be studied and the significance this material has within general education, which includes intellectual, physical, emotional and social factors. For example, we give tremendous importance to sports. I think, in the long run, the country will have good athletes."

Or physically healthy people, I thought. Sports were very important because in the integral development of man it must be recognized that we have a body to take care of and to develop, and that it is the physiological substratum of all behavior. To believe that someday our small country would become the world champion of something ... there was a long distance to go yet, many other priorities to consider.

"We believe in self-education," continued the teacher, an attractive woman of twenty-five. "We believe that nobody can really teach anything to anyone. It is necessary to develop skills, *that one learns how to learn*. This self-education on every level is the goal of the school. In reality, it's self-education for freedom."

"For freedom? Well, all this seems quite planned and, as it has been said so many times, nothing should be left to fate. Operant conditioning involves much in control, not in freedom, which simply seems to be a linguistic problem and a heavy load that we've inherited from previous eras. Freedom is a myth. The more one thinks about it, the more one realizes it. So then how can you be sure that we're training men and women to be free?"

"They make many decisions. They know the consequences of their actions. They know that things have effects, results, lead to something. Behavior doesn't exist in a void; it has history behind it; it acts according to an environment; it produces *consequences* that may affect the probability of its repetition. Positive consequences cause—"

"Yes," interrupted Felipe, who had just arrived from the garden, bringing a rose to the teacher. "Let's go inside, I want to see what's happening at the fifth grade children's council."

The children's council was evaluating the performance of schoolmates, including school grades, friendships, moral education, creativity, sport activities and group spirit. All very difficult to evaluate and operationalize, I thought; all were very mentalist and diversified. Besides, what do children know about the goals of the New Era, about what is right and wrong for man?

"Are you married?" I asked the teacher, although it was irrelevant. "You know a lot about children but you seem very young."

"Yes, I am married. I have two children in kindergarten. I work here half a day and dedicate the rest of the day to my children and my husband."

So there still existed "traditional" families, with fathers, mothers and children. Women still existed who took care of their husbands and children. Beautiful! Hopefully this would never be lost. With so many innovations in the family structure, I thought that traditional couples had disappeared completely.

The children's council was judging a little classmate who had been absent for several days because he had gone for a walk. He had missed a module of mathematics which integrated between the preceding and the following modules, in such a way that it would be difficult for him to catch up to the level of his mates. In the council there were rewards and punishments (costs response programs) for groups as well as *individuals*. A "lazy" child like this one was going to affect the level of all his classmates. The punishment was going to fall on the whole group. This was terrible and implied that the grup could not take the excursion of ornithology on F day in order to observe the construction patterns of tropical birds' nests. They were greatly interested in this, but by sufficiently lowering the point level of the group, they definitely were not going to be able to go. The whole group was going to suffer the adverse consequences of a lazy student who preferred to go for a walk during school days rather than attend mathematics classes.

"Do you recognize that your inappropriate behavior seriously affected all your classmates?" the group leader, a boy of twelve, solemnly asked. He was mature for his age and had a serious expression on his face.

The "accused" did not say anything but made an affirmative nod with his head.

"Do you think it's correct?"

The boy gave a negative response with his head.

"Well, then, what alternative do you suggest? What's your solution to our problem?"

"I'm going to study more and I'll take another exam on mathematics," said the accused in a broken voice. "If two of you help me, I think I can bring myself up to date and take the exam next week. In this way we can all go on the ornithological excusion next F day."

"Very well. Which of you would like to help our friend in mathematics? I need two volunteers to go over set theory. In order to compensate for lost time, this will be done in free time."

Two little girls raised their hands almost simultaneously and both received the assignment of helping their companion with mathematics.

"Everything works like this—the teacher explained to me. "It's considered that disciplinary problems can be solved on a group level and the cildren take this very seriously. Of course, the day will come when all discipline problems will disappear because everyone will be so sufficiently conditioned that no one will attempt to escape to the country instead of studying mathematics. But that day still hasn't arrived."

"I think this process of public judgment, of evaluation by schoolmates causes an anxious situation and produces unnecessary guilt feelings."

"I don't know. Anyway the process should also be evaluated and we will do it during meditation time at the end of the year. Nothing is fixed and inviolable. All this is science and, therefore, is subject to error and correction. The creation of guilt feelings in the children is something we try to avoid at all costs. On the contrary, we want to have happy and creative children who develop their emotions and social relationships, who discover science for themselves instead of mechanically learning it with the help of teaching machines."

"A mixture of the Montessori method and operant conditioning. Do you believe it works well?"

"I do. A definite evaluation still had to be done. I forgot about the system of socialization—or humanization—that has proven to be efficient and also becomes the children's responsibility. When a child enters the school a group 'adopts' him and initiates him into all the formal and informal requirements of the institution. The older children bring and take home the smaller ones, play with them at school and afterwards, they show them social norms and new games. They assimilate them into the world of adults. In the most common cases a group of advanced children, let's say the fourth grade, adopts the little ones of the first grade. They serve as older brothers and sisters to them and fulfill a tremendously important role. This system has been evaluated and its efficiency has been demonstrated. It's an educational innovation that's going to have great meaning. Life is with people, you know. And the most relevant people to one's life is someone like ones ownself; in this case, children who resemble other children. Education should be stimulated by schoolmates not by teachers. No one can educate anyone, but the little classmates can help greatly so that each child educates himself."

CHAPTER 17
CAN SCIENCE SAVE US?

Our reputation as a "scientific" society originated in the election of our country as the seat of an International Congress of Engineering and Applied Sciences. We had sought this event in order that the experts of our country could present before the eyes of the world the widely discussed basis of social engineering upon which the New Era was being built. In most cases, when something was published about us it was negative. This always seemed strange to me. Had we not eliminated misery, illiteracy and unemployment? Were we not in the process of wiping out physical and mental illnesses? Did we not have truly innovative family, educational and work systems? Nevertheless, criticisms remained: the society was defective because it had been planned. The worst thing about us is that we had left nothing to chance: everything was planned; the environment was organized; human behavior was programmed.

The discussion continued *ad infinitum,* but it was a very stale discussion that amounted to little. I did not like to waste my time and that is why I avoided such eternal groundless discussions. But most people loved this. Therefore, in the Congress of Engineering and Applied Sciences it was possible to discuss hour after hour the topics of control and freedom, of social planning, of handling human behavior. It was sufficient reason for me not to attend such a congress.

At the inauguration, Martin gave the plenary address. For this reason all of his collaborators in National Planning had to attend, whether they wanted to or not. Since I had begun to accept the principles which we had loudly preached, I though it better for me to enjoy doing something I had to do; to smile during difficult times. It was necessary to learn to like what we had to like.

"In the New Era, science held a place of great importance within the organization of society," Mr. President said with great solemnity. "Ours is a scientific society. We interpret science as an attitude of looking for the facts rather than worrying about what has been said about those facts. We ask questions about nature and await her answers. It's important that the questions are well formulated, in order to understand the language of nature; it's essential that the answers are relevant to our previous knowledge. We are not a nation of politicians, but a nation of scientists. We test all our reforms to evaluate and change them if it's necessary. Then we compare our premises with reality, and if they differ we modify them. We have a profound respect for nature, as well as human nature."

The great conference hall was filled, and Martin's speech was being translated simultaneously into English and French. I think Martin had drunk half a bottle of vodka before getting on the podium and, for this reason, he seemed to talk with security and self-confidence. His alcoholism worried me but I had never broached the subject with him. After all, the lives of the New Era programmers were full of pressures, stress, and tremendous responsibilities. Each one of us tried to find and escape, a way to eliminate anxiety. Alcohol was a bad road, I was convinced of that. But I did not criticize Martin for drinking, as long as it was in moderation.

"We believe that a scientific attitude is an objective one, within certain limits. We're convinced that the scientist isn't a cold and passive observer of nature but a passionate hunter of order, of logic, of universal meaning. In a certain way the scientist resembles the profoundly religious man in search of universal significance. We consider that by observing the world, the scientist is altering it; he selects events from reality and formulates them into theories. These really aren't a consequence of observation but are its foundation. In other words, the theory tells us what we should look for. Scientists are passionate men, full of prejudices just like anybody else."

"Neither do we believe that science is a game. We think it's an institution too important to be considered a game. We take seriously Popper and Kuhn; we believe in paradigms. We believe that the history of science hasn't terminated yet. Rather, we think it's just beginning. For countries like ours, with limited means and big projects of social changes, science must be helpful. We're in favor of basic scientific research and we give it all the support it deserves. But we emphasize applied science, since our problems are urgent and can't wait for solutions to be found through laboratory investigations. We apply what exists, take data from laboratory investigations, determine rules of correspondence with human and social reality, and apply actual information, although it may be incomplete. We even improvise whenever necessary..."

I do not think Martin should have said that. Certainly we were improvising a lot, but it was not necessary to mention it in front of an international audience that might misinterpret it. I would have liked to have written his speech instead of letting him do it.

"In talking about science I don't refer only to physical science, but to all sciences. I believe the distinction between natural sciences and social or human sciences is nothing more than an anachronism. We know today that man and his society are part of nature; therefore we believe in just one science. We think some sciences are *further* developed than others; for example physics, which has always been in the vanguard. Let's say, there are *developed* and underdeveloped sciences, instead of natural sciences and social sciences."

Without a doubt this should please the engineers and physicists, given than they have always believed that the road followed by physics is the only alternative for all sciences. Which is very debatable, Mr. President. Anyway, we will talk about the subject another time, I thought.

"This science, which encompasses everything from atoms to galaxies, from metabolic transformations to cultural changes, is one of the pillars of our society. The other pillar concerns itself with *respect for man and his well-being*. We're followers of humanism in a new sense, of scientific humanism, not of literary humanism. We do things instead of simply talking about them. For this it's necessary to take risks, to improvise and to make amendments.

"Not too long ago," continued Mr. President, "the National Science Foundation of the United States discussed the scope of the advance of information processing which began with the microcircuit computers. Economic computers with abilities beyond the human imagination are becoming a reality. Systems of information handling are accessible to the ordinary man. At first a commercial 'microchip' could store 16,000 functions, now it can store over 160,000. This tremendous technological advance in the handling of information implies, just like Gutenberg's printing press, the mechanization of information. We're standing at the door of a technological revolution of great magnitude, of variables combination, data analysis, accessible to anyone. a revolution in neurology, spectography of infrared rays, cristalography of X-rays and investigation on a microstructure scale await us."

"Why haven't these changes come to psycology, sociology, and anthropology? Because the conceptual framework of these sciences are very complex and demand a large quantity of interaction processes between the variables. Besides, the progress in these disciplines, in psychology for example, has been blocked by the limiting power of traditional mathematics and the mental process it requires. Thanks to the changes in information processing, the theory of behavioral sciences could encompass the whole complexity of the phenomena that we are trying to understand."

"We're told that our society is based solely *on psychology*," observed Martin after taking a sip of water, although I think he would have preferred a sip of vodka. "In reality we base ourselves in all the sciences. We've created Institutes of Investigation for Longevity, Cancer Control, and Family Studies. We have big laboratories for classical and operant conditioning which, for the most part, are run by national scientists. The Criminology Institute has done magnificent research. We don't await many new developments in astronomy or quantum physics, but we do in economics, sociology and anthropology.

"By believing in an unified science, we've given a lot of importance to behavioral psychology. Kantor said that all sciences studied overt behavior. Therefore, speaking of behavioral psychology is the same as talking about scientific psychology. What must be changed in order to make a new society is *man*. In most utopias, be they of Plato, Sir Thomas More, Aldous Huxley, George Orwell, or even B. F. Skinner, the necessity to change man has been explicitly recognized. A new image can't be created using old and deteriorated materials. The role of psychology is to develop a new man, and the philosophical framework upon which we base ourselves is the framework of science and humanism. A science that starts with man, that's made by man, that must serve man."

After Mr. President's speech, other people began to speak. Fortunately I was not among them, since I had managed to invent an excuse beforehand to avoid speaking. Afterwards followed the required cocktail party, during which Martin, after such a long wait, could drink his vodka. The President of Congress, a brilliant specialist in systems engineering from the Soviet Union, came up and said to me in English:

"Now I understand the very long and rough road you have before you. It's quite complex, this idea of changing man and society through behavioral science and humanism. Now I understand the meaning of a phrase on many posters which are distributed all over the city, whose message is also heard on radio and television: 'We have a lot to do, and we are doing it.'"

CHAPTER 18
THE PLACE OF RELIGION

"Science can't save us," I explained to my friend the Soviet engineer, while taking a tour of the city during the International Congress of Engineering and Applied Sciences. "Really, I believe nothing can save us, neither science, nor religion, nor politics. Each one of has to save himself."

'Save himself from what?" he asked, with a rather good command of English. Nevertheless, I felt he had misunderstood me.

"Save himself from an empty, meaningless life, in which time passes, youth becomes distant and one becomes only a spectator of history. Let me explain. People need to transcend their own limits, to give meaning to their existence, to escape from death. In the Soviet Union I think this is done through science, if I'm not wrong. A tremendous importance is given to science. The scientific explanation of the world and the theological explanation of the world are forever at odds, in order to demonstrate that religion and superstition are the same thing."

"Yes, that's right. We strongly insist on atheism. Tell me, Professor González, are all of you atheists?"

"A difficult question, my friend. If by that you mean not belonging to any formal religion, not believing in miracles but in universal principles, in thinking that the world is a result of evolution and not creation, then, we're really atheists. But if by that you mean that we don't believe man will transcend his own limits, give meaning to his life, look for what is beyond himself, then we aren't athiests. In a religious sense we are atheists; in a psychological sense we are not. There is a test of values, I think by Allport and others, that measures religious values as the need to transcend, to give meaning to existence, to go beyond everyday and transitory life. The new man we are forming will have, without a doubt, a high religious rating on this test. In other words, we are a profoundly religious society. Religion means *religation*, to unite oneself to others, to unite things so that they don't crumble. We don't worship anyone: neither gods, nor men. We believe that it's equally probable that the Egyptian and Greek gods existed, as well as the Jewish God."

"In the manner of Bertrand Russell and his justification for not being a Christian," said the Soviet engineer.

"The fact that we don't worship any God doesn't mean that we believe life ends here and now. Think of man's profound ignorance, of the little progress of science, of the great gaps in our knowledge. Think that human history is just beginning."

"That doesn't give anyone the right to justify pseudoexplanations, superstitions or magical explanations of the world. In the USSR. we allow religion but we have antireligious propaganda and atheist education. If someone wants to be religious, let him, it's his problem; in reality, only the older people are. The young and intelligent people are proud to be atheists. To a great extent, I think your society resembles ours: a similar school system, a centralized economic planning. We both talk of social changes, goals to be achieved, as well as the formation of a new man with scientific aid. It's curious that you don't admit that you are building a socialist society. You've listed Marx as one of the ten greatest men in all history, and gave his name to one of the ten months of the year."

"We also dedicated a month to Jesus."

"Yes, I know, and it deeply puzzles me. You resemble us a lot; your society is similar to ours. Maybe you use a wider and more modern concept of science that the USSR, because for us 'science' is almost only physics. But in religion we differ greatly."

"I think we're less harsh and demanding with our people," I observed. "We are a *permissive* society that emphasizes reward rather than punishment; that allows everyone to participate in government decisions. Ours is a society *focused on children* and infancy, a scientific society, but also a human one."

"And science isn't human? Listen. I think we're talking about the same thing. Let's clarify one important point. You have a pluralist society, an 'open society,' and that's very difficult to handle. The day will come when you will 'close' it: you won't allow criticism; won't let people leave the country; you will control the incoming and outgoing information. An open society is a luxury in which only the capitalists can indulge. Do you know why? Because only seven percent of the population own seventy percent of the wealth of the entire planet. This economy of abundance, of consumption and waste, allows them to have an open society. These people like such a system. If they leave the country, they return; they criticize the government, but the balance of points for and against is always favourable. In the rest of the world we can't afford this luxury of having an open society. It's a matter of economics, just as Marx said . . ."

"Perhaps. Meanwhile, we're going to maintain our *open* society, as you say, and as I think Popper said—a society with criticism, changes, permanent evaluation, and participation of the masses in government decisions. But also a society in which we respect but don't encourage religion."

"Strange, quite strange. I'll never understand why you've maintained religions when you could have freed yourselves from them. The scientific explanation of the world which you defend so much here is absolutely incompatible with superstition, magic, and, of course, religion. Do you have religious ceremonies, dogmas, orders, cults? Do people go to church each Sunday, I mean, each F day?"

"Those who wish to, go. Churches can hold services but religious propaganda is prohibited. Religion is considered an individual matter. We respect religion but we don't encourage it. Would you like to see a religious ceremony?"

"Of course! It could be fun. I promise I won't ridicule what I see. I'll observe everything with the scientific eyes of an anthropologist, as if I'm watching a primitive African or Latin American tribal ceremony."

Eventually we arrived at the city zone that was on holiday and entered into a temple. It was a somber, classic construction, with Ionic columns and white walls; everything was simultaneously elegant and simple. A group of people was listening to a woman speaking. The woman was dressed in white from head to feet, with her arms bare. Perhaps the bare arms were because of the heat, or maybe she wanted to imitate a priestess of some oriental religion. She spoke with passion and it was difficult to translate for my friend all she was saying. She spoke of brotherhood, of the misery in the world, of children dying from hunger, and of diseases all over the planet. She referred to women with illegitimate children who were ostracized by their families and society, and ended up working as maids in homes of the rich. There they suffered unlimited humiliations, and the raising of their illegitimate children became an indescribable horror. While she cleaned, washed and cooked, her child cried or often burned himself on the spot of boiling soup as he ran around the kitchen. The woman had no money for medical services. The child's cries of pain mixed with the mother's tears of anguish.

"Not a very pretty picture," commented my Soviet friend.

"She says this happens all over the world, especially in the Third World which constitutes two thirds of the planet. It's the normal living pattern; humanity has controlled diseases but people don't have money to control misery, malnutrition, social injustices, emptiness, ignorance, all the sorrows of the world. I hope she mentions that thanks to science and humanism we've been able to control those social diseases."

"Einstein at Princeton. Al the pain of the world. And the emptiness, the terrifying emptiness everywhere . . ."

The woman talked about that mother who could not give to her own child the milk reserved for her master's children. She had to tie up her child with wire all day long. Her child suffered arrogance and maltreatment from the rich children. Each time she was suspected of giving milk to her own little one she suffered humiliation and shame. Because she had a child she received a low salary. Finding another job as a maid was impossible because of her child. She had to protect the job she had, until the lady of the house decided to throw her out as a "lowly servant" without prior notice or any compensation.

The audience was really moved. I stopped translating for my friend. The "priestess" raised her arms, shouted and sang. The crowd followed her, singing, shouting, crying. The grief of others, of those children, mistreated and burned, malnourished and abandoned, victims of social injustices, of those women struggling for survival, alone and abandoned, had touched the people to the bone. I turned to my friend and saw him frowning and watery-eyed. Incredible. Soviet engineers, leaders of the world's most serious societies, are also moved by a child of the Third World who burns himself trying to grab a pot of boiling soup on the fire.

"Einstein at Princeton. All the pain of the world. And the emptiness, the terrifying emptiness everywhere...."

Music was heard, lights and colors were seen. The music was turned up. It was strong and shrill. There were many multicolored lights.

> You left me by the wayside, you took my hope with you....
> When the wheat was most golden in the earth of my soul....
> One sunny morning, spring sang....
> But in seeing the house without you,
> My whole body cried....
> One sunny morning, on the beach I waited for you.
> The sea that took you away,
> to never bring you back....

The crowd sang, danced, turned around in circles. We followed the crowd. The priestess looked like a crazy person with her arms raised, shouting, singing. Soon the whole temple was filled with our voices, our dances and our songs. I found myself submerged in this tumult, imitating the actions of everyone. I looked for my friend and saw him doing the same. He sang and cried too, like a native countryman, as if he had been born in our tropical country and felt in his bones all the human misery, the controllable evils, the injustices, all the grief of the whole world....

> One sunny morning, spring sang....
> But in seeing the house without you, my whole body cried....
> You are my childhood song, the cry of my guitar....
> And upon the sea that keeps you,
> I bring you French roses
> and the cry of my guitar ...

from these eyes weeping for you,
from this friend singing for you. . . .

The ceremony continued for hours. God was not once mentioned. They did not consume drugs or inhale incense. After the dances people sat on the floor and in silence took each others hands and listened to a beautiful lyric poem, profoundly philosophical and human. I tried to translate it for my friend but I think he, as well as I, was too saturated by the dance, the songs, the shouts, what we had just seen and experienced. The poem talked of what this new temple of humanity was: without gods, dogmas, precepts, cults, but profoundly religious, being a part of humanity, solving the human anguish of loneliness. After all, religion originally meant *re-litigation* and this is what we were doing at this moment, joining the humble people of the world, with the distant and obscure people, all of our brothers and sisters of this planet. Definitely, "my kingdom is of this world. . ."

"A place where people from every class and condition can join hands, love, dance, worship, sing or cry together. A place that believes in the survival of every man, in other men, and in death. A place that speaks the language of music. A place for young and old, women and men, beauty and ugliness, believers and atheists. A place that aspires to human well-being as its ultimate goal. A place that just now turns into reality. . . ."

CHAPTER 19
NEITHER MARX NOR JESUS

"Man created God in his own image," my Soviet friend said a couple of days later. "The attitude of the Greek gods toward life was typical of this people. Likewise was that of the Jewish God conceived by a few men who lived a rough existence in a hostile, desert environment. Jesus was an empire builder. The kingdom he created extended throughout the world and settled down in Ceasars' Rome. The emperor Constantine was the one who helped him to "officialize" it. The same occurred with Marx, an other Jew who, like Jesus, also had messianic ideas. He, too, was persecuted and rehabilitated after his death and resurrection."

"Marx and Jesus. . . ."

"Two Jews who decided to conquer the world and did it. Marx's empire began in 1917. It has marched around the world with giant steps. If you extrapolate the growth curve of Marxism, you might come to the conclusion that within a short time it will enclose the whole planet. It's simply a matter of time and statistics, of extrapolation of graphic data."

World communism, its accelerated growth and the analogy between Marx and Jesus, were topics that gave us a lot to think about for several hours. Along with the problem of religion and man's "inherent need" for it.

"Organized religion has changed greatly. What yesterday was considered heresy, a deed worthy of hanging for today is common practice. What isn't accepted today, for example the marriage of Catholic priests, tomorrow will be a common norm. In this aspect the Church has changed; all churches have changed. Actually, they change because they have no choice. It's a matter of survival, of adapting to the environment in order to keep alive. Darwin was right. Species and institutions adapt themselves to the environment by changing, to prevent their extinction. It's the law of life, the survival of the fittest. Of the fittest for what? Of the fittest to survive!"

"Religion has changed tremendously. I think Marxism has had much to do with it, especially with respect to Latin America. The Church and communism have united their efforts in an attempt to offer alternatives to solving the problems of the continent, something that would have seemed impossible to do. Revolutionary priests abound in spite of the sacred wrath of the bishops," I pointed out.

"But this approach is dangerous. I think it's going to harm Marxists as well as Catholics. You know, Marxism has also undergone a transformation adapting itself to the needs of each country and every historical circumstance. It's quite different to talk of Marxism in the USSR, in Italy or in Chile. They're different realities, although they're based on the same principles. The Chinese, as you know, accuse us of being 'revisionists' and of having separated from the pure Marxist principles. Similarly many orthodox Catholics accuse the advance churches of separating from God. Both religions, of Marx and of Jesus, have conservative and progressive features."

"From a psychological point of view I believe religion has a place in man's life. Religion without revelation, dogmas, orders or cults; without superstition or pseudoexplanations of the world; a religion that relinquishes any scientific authority to pass judgment on matters of astronomy, evolution, psychology or sociology. For example, today birth control is a controversial subject among scientists and Catholics. Not so long ago it was the evolution of the species, and before that it was the earth's revolution around the sun. In *all* polemics between science and religion, science reigns victorious. Science has always won. There's no exception to this. Today the polemic between science and religion doesn't lie in astronomy or biology but in demography. What the Catholics say is the contrary to what the demographers say. As in the preceding cases science will probably win."

"And in the long run, religion will say that she wasn't 'really' fully understood and that she really never said that the sun revolved around the earth, that the species were changeless or that it was necessary to avoid birth control," observed my Soviet friend.

"In spite of this I believe there's a place for religion within society, not magical religion, but the kind that enables us to unify with humanity, the one that helps us to transcend our own limits."

"And which one is that? No, I don't agree with you. I believe it's better to completely free ourselves from religion. It's too dangerous to have around; and it's an enigma to me how you've given it a place in the New Era. If I were a leader in this country I would eliminate religion once and for all. I think future generations would be eternally grateful to me for that."

"I don't know, I'm not sure. There are many things in life that we haven't explained, realities that have to be coped with. Man's most serious problem is death. Although science may succeed in lengthening life and making it more worthwhile, there will always be that moment of death. We're condemned to die. Men and women who are now on this planet, in twenty or thirty more years will die. There are illnesses, injustices, pains and miseries—all the negative facets of life that have been with us since history began. For instance you're told that you have cancer and you're going to die within three months. How do you give meaning to what remains of your life? What rational and mature explanation do you find to answer why this has happened to you? Why necessarily me? Why? Why? There's no answer. In a different situation, your little daughter walks down the street, a bus runs over her and she dies instantly. What can you do? How do you find strength to go on living? There are many things that aren't explained by science alone."

"Religion and science, as well as literature and philosophy, operate from different levels of explanation. It's dangerous to confuse these levels."

"Of course. I want my people to have a way of escaping pain and anguish, the existential dilemma that always weighs us down. Whatever can be solved by science, fine, we'll use science for man's benefit. But many other things remain to be discussed at another level. I think if we took religion away from people, prophets would probably arise and religion would be reborn; or even worse, people would turn to drugs and alcohol."

"So God isn't dead and Nietzsche was wrong?"

"In many countries we observe a rebirth of religion in young people. It's difficult to explain. No, it's not a strengthening of traditional religions. It's a return to the oriental ones, especially in search for unity with nature. The so-called "children of Christ" aren't the worst young people of Europe and the United States. On the contrary, they're intelligent, sensitive people, who are looking for universal meaning. That's all I want to say. Let's get rid of stratified religion, of the traditional hierarchy that followed the pattern of the Roman Caesars. Good-bye to pseudoexplanations of the world, to polemics between science and religion in which science always wins. Good-bye to superstitions, to ignorance. But not to the psychological foundation of religion, not to the harmony among men, to the need for universal meaning."

"After all, it was Newton who observed that a scientist is like a child gathering shells on a beach, while in front of him the unknown sea stretches toward infinity."

CHAPTER 20
THE EXPERIMENTAL ANALYSIS

In spite of liking this search for universal values, of this integration of emotional factors to the quest of giving a meaning to life, to me science remained the most valuable and appropriate method for studying the world. I wrote this in an article sent to the newspapers for the fourth anniversary of our psychological and social revolution. It was important that people thought about these things, of what science is, and what it is not. Obviously, the scientist is like a child gathering shells on the shores of the unknown. But it is not enough just to stand in front of that immense sea and sigh, thinking of all that we do not know. It is better to devote ourselves to collecting the shells, to studying what we do know, to classifying and organizing that knowledge. I insisted on that as a subject for meditation at the end of the year for our readers.

"Our society is a scientific society," I stated in my writing. "The New Era is based on scientific assumptions and is as strong and solid as scientific methodology. It clearly distinguishes what is science, philosophy, literature and even religion. It doesn't mix values. It avoids going from one level of explanation to another without clarifying the correspondence rules. It avoids extrapolations. In a strict sense, science is a search for order. It is an intent to describe relationships between facts. If description precedes the facts, we speak of 'prediction'; if it follows, we speak of 'explanation.' In both cases, the importance of science lies in understanding the universe and its control. Exact and valid functional laws make the control easier. If we are able to produce a phenomenon, we can truthfully say that we understand it."

"Man is part of the universe. He is a product of the same laws that gave rise to other beings and is found in the same line of evolution as other species. Reflecting on the universe, and understanding it, does not mean that we are not subject to the same laws which govern the rest of the world. Human behavior is no mystery. It exists in time and space just like stars or amoebas."

"Nevertheless, the study of behavior has been especially difficult and slow. This is due to the complexity of behavior and to the fact that we find ourselves too close to it; we are so close that we cannot study it objectively, like the trees that prohibit us from seeing the forest."

I was pondering all this when I received a call from Martin who urgently wanted to see me. I interrupted what I was trying to write for the newspapers and went up to his office located two floors above mine in the Presidential Palace. Mr. President had just closed the Congress on Engineering and Applied Sciences and was anxious to return to his normal work. I had taken my friend, the Soviet engineer, to the airport and promised to send him a couple of books on scientific psychology where experimental analysis of behavior and its application to our social reform were discussed in detail. I thought the articles I was writing for the national newspapers could be useful to them since they were quite ignorant about operant psychology. After all, only now in the USSR, were these topics beginning to be studied. To talk to them about the *behavioral* level of explanation without having to reduce it to physiology, is something alien to Pavlov's and Bechterev's followers. Fortunately Vygostsky also existed who set up the basis for an autonomous psychology without having to reduce it to physiology as Pavlov would have liked. But using Skinner's psychology for social change was something equally fascinating and unknown to the Soviets.

"Dave, it's nice to see you. How are you? I haven't heard from you for a long time. We have a lot to do. I just received a project from the Commission on Delinquency and I want your opinion before we try it. Besides, there is the work from the Commission on Recreation that has to be reevaluated."

"Like you, I was at the Congress on Engineering. It's not easy to work and be a tourist guide at the same time. I accompanied the president of the Congress to several places, among them a temple on last F day. He found it strange and fascinating, although in his opinion it would be better to get rid of religion entirely. We went to other places, including schools and collective farms. I think our social reform made a good impression on him."

"I suppose you didn't go to one of the Sexual Health Centers."

"No! That's all we would need! You know I always insist on not taking foreigners to such places. Had I done that I'm afraid the Russians would have asked for political asylum in our country! Those Soviets are puritanical and old-fashioned, you know. It's funny how they can be so advanced in science, investigate so many important things and, at the same time, consider that human behavior isn't an area for scientific study, that it's immutable, that there exists an unchangeable 'human nature,' etc. I think we could teach them many things and, at the same time, learn a lot from them."

"Yes, man, it's true. In general I liked the Congress; it had wide national and international coverage. I think we made a good impression. I'm getting old, my friend, and I believe a person should have one gratification or another in his lifetime. Do you want a drink?"

"No, thanks. But if you want to fix yourself one, don't worry about me. I think you did very well emphasizing the role of psychology in the New Era in your inaugural speech."

"Have a drink, man. Don't let me drink alone. Here you are."

I drank my Scotch without a word and we continued to analyze the work we had in front of us. Martin dedicated very little time to his family. He was always with us and I figured his wife and five children must have resented it. It was quite a demanding job being president of the nation and having to change the whole social system.

Back in my office I continued writing my articles. I wanted to explain the concept of reinforcement, the importance of understanding behavior and its modification, reinforcement schedules, everything that is required in the experimental analysis of behavior. I pointed out that operant principles made new strategies of investigation easier without considering the traditional problems of experimental design. Research on operant conditioning has been carried out without paying attention to traditional psychological problems, neither to its methods nor its theories. Nevertheless, experimental analysis is no longer thought of as a "school," an island, a system. There has been an attempt to integrate it within psychology as a whole, especially within experimental psychology. Many problems that Skinner and his followers never dealt with are worked on today. The specialists are not as worried about the "purity" of the methods nor the proposed conceptualizations. Limits have really widened.

Operant behavior is studied by organizing things in such a way that an organism's behavior affects its environment in someway. For example: a rat that presses a lever in one of Skinner's boxes or a pigeon that pecks a disk. This response is considered part of everything done by an organism; just as behavior is divided into relatively arbitrary units called responses, environment is divided into relatively arbitrary units called stimuli. In a strict sense, operant psychology is not a psychology of stimulus-response but a stimulus-response-consequence psychology. If the organism's response modifies the environment in such a way that it obtains the desired consequence (water, food, escape from electric shock), it will learn the response. The consequence as a reinforcement is defined by such modification. The relationship between the response and the consequence is called response-reinforcement contingency. Reinforcement schedules have been devised and their study has originated a highly sophisticated behavioral engineering. It can be considered the area of psychology with the highest development level. Whatever criterion we use to define this level, the experimental analysis of behavior, specifically the study of reinforcement schedules, is a very advanced branch of contemporary science.

The big difference that exists between laboratory findings in experimental analysis of behavior and its applications to behavior modification, has always surprised me. It is a gigantic gap. I do not think we are applying even one percent of our findings. "Physics" (laboratory work) is light years away from "engineering" (behavior modification) and probably many complex problems in human behavior will be solved once complex reinforcement programs are applied rather than the simple ones, of fixed-ratio, variable-ratio, fixed-interval or variable-interval. Human behavior is very complicated and, without a doubt, is mediated by quite complex reinforcement programs. This analysis will be done someday . . . someday.

In my newspaper articles I also thought it was appropriate to mention recent developments that had changed the panorama for behavioral study, for example, the influence of ethology, of auto-shaping and of behavioral contrasts. In auto-shaping it had been discovered that the behavior of an organism can generate or maintain itself through classical contingencies. This inspired studies on the interaction between Pavlovian and Skinnerian, classical and operant conditioning.

The boundaries of learning, which have worried ethologists and their followers within operant psychology, have demonstrated that the selection of a specific reinforcement, response or stimulus, can prevent the selection of others that are effective with such reinforcement, response or stimulus. Organisms have innate preference for certain behaviors; they also prefer certain reinforcements and stimuli. Thus, taken from ethology, and without much preparation, the concept of "species-specific behavior" was introduced, which seems to be nothing more than the old concept of "instinct" dressed in a new wardrobe and with a more elegant name.

Another relatively recent development was associated with the work of Premack, a highly creative man whom I would have liked to bring to Panama. He insists that reinforcements do not have absolute qualities, but that these are functionally defined and determined through situations; even reward and punishment can be the result of some programmed contingencies. It is important to consider the operant baseline and its interaction with other fundamental processes when the conditioned suppression is obtained in aversive situations.

Research exists on physiological and motivational processes, for example, related to food and water consumption and to the maintenance of a stable temperature. Thermoregulated behavioral mechanisms are very important. At a perceptual process level, great advance has been reached in the so-called animal psychophysics, which supposedly was an area "impossible" to study because the psychophysics of Fechner was based on introspection and verbal reports, by the subject. Animal psychophysics was impossible since we cannot expect animals to use introspection or verbal reports. But today it exists, thanks to Skinner and experimental analysis of behavior.

CHAPTER 21
THE EXPERIMENTAL SYNTHESIS

The field of experimental analysis had grown a great deal but I do not think we would have "surpassed" Skinner as some people said. I believe we are working within the guidelines he established. Today we are dedicated to much more extensive problems than those that interested Skinner; psychophysiology, perception and cognitive processes have profitted from operant methods. Successful attempts have been made to applying such concepts and methods to the study of social behavior. In Mexico and the United States, communities exist like Walden Two. Only we have dared to apply experimental analysis *at the national level,* in a country that existed here and now. Without a doubt, our Walden Three was one of the principal places where experimental analysis of behavior has been applied. Its success or failure was going to generate long reaching implications for applied behavioral analysis.

"Skinner's box has done for psychology what the telescope did for astronomy or the microscope for biology," I explained to Mr. President in one of our National Planning meetings. "It permitted environmental control in such a way that each behavioral effect could be studied in detail with minimum mistakes. Response rate has done for psychology what reflex did for physiology: the analysis unit which is the basic element upon which the whole structure of science is built, in one case, psychology, in the other physiology. From this point of view, Skinner is to psychology what Sechenov was to physiology.

"Obviously, experimental analysis of behavior should originate an experimental *synthesis* of behavior," I said. "Analysis is the division of elements into basic units, functional units of behavior or triple contingency of stimulus-response-reinforcement. These must be integrated in order to explain complex behavioral processes, man's relationship to his environment, social interaction. The experimental synthesis of behavior is the next big step in the study of psychology. It will not imply an 'improvement' of experimental behavioral analysis. That's not what I mean to say. It will imply broader limits, more complex mathematical patterns, extrapolation of data and integration of theories of broad explanatory capacity. The experimental synthesis of behavior is the next big step."

The whole National Planning group was together, preparing the end-of-the-year documents. I think we had progressed considerably. Even the economy seemed to have improved. We still had to work more at the international level to restore respect of Walden Three around the world. In spite of our efforts, any final evaluations published about tour huge social experiment were negative. Why? Because there was a Department of National Planning that really made big decisions. Because there were commissions on Education, Health, Human Development, Social Communication, Family and Sexuality, Economy, and many other areas that were in charge of the social planification; because there were guidelines that were taken seriously and annual plans that were executed. Because we were a *planned* society. We could make a lot of progress, eliminate many traditional human illnesses; but we were looked upon unfavorably because we did not believe in "freedom" but in control; we did not believe in "self-determination" but in managing the environment to control individual behavior. What could be done to attain a more positive international image for our Walden Three?

"I really don't care what they think of us," Martin said to me after I had expressed my concern. "Facts speak for themselves and I don't care if they ridicule and criticize us. David, you know they say that I'm a drunk and a paranoic, that I'm selfish and have messianic fantasies?"

What a correct description of our president, I thought, but obviously restrained myself from verbalizing it. One advantage of man is that he can internalize his speech in such a way that he can "think" without moving the phonetic muscles. It is wonderful being able to talk to ourselves. Obviously, we introverts do it more than the extroverts.

"They forget that we've wiped out misery, illiteracy, over-population and many physical and mental illnesses. In these four years we've advanced considerably and turned humanity's most desired dreams into reality. An equalized society, without social classes, where everyone can truly have a quality life. We've done it with the help of science, and that arouses envy in people. We have enemies in China, the USSR and the United States. I distrust the United States more than the other powers. Do you know why? Because the North Americans really know the importance of behavioral science in order to reach social objectives and political goals."

"Only in the United States and Canada have behavioral sciences attained a high level of development," I pointed out.

"True, man. Oh! I forgot something important. There's a young North American who wants to work with us, and I would like you to read his curriculum and interview him. He has a fabulous training in behavioral science and could be very helpful. We don't usually accept personally unknown people into the National Planning group who haven't previously proved their loyalty. We're a closed society in this sense. Our group is cautious since we have so many enemies and have to avoid any mistakes."

"Who is this North American?"

"His name is Charles Powell. He studied at Yale, I believe anthropology and psychology. He's worked with the United States government, I think in the army, and has a brilliant record. He's well prepared and has an excellent group spirit. He speaks Spanish very well. I'll send him around for you to interview. He's interested in working with any commissions in National Planning."

"I'll interview him. Send him to my office the day after tomorrow."

I could not see him earlier because of previous engagements. We spent far too much time in meetings and more meetings. We had to analyze reform projects, write evaluations, read the commission's reports. I had to talk with the coordinators of each commission, meet with the full commission and finally, attend the General Council of National Planning. Added to this were my interminable conversations with Mr. President. If Martin were a little more concrete and if he drank less, and allowed me to drink less.... If he would confine himself to the questions of the day, I think we could have made better use of our time. I sometimes grew tired of those long meetings, of sitting for hours in the ultramodern central hall listening to someone presenting data and curves. The lecturer passed slides, discussed his data, explained points of growth, analyzed the cost-benefit relationship, the ideological and psychological meanings of the project, and opened the discussion. Like the "good children" we were, we had read the documents beforehand. Or perhaps better said, like people who had suffered the torture and dehumanizing process of graduate school and had learned to do what was expected of us.

I would have liked to have had a reliable assistant. But since I handled confidential, "dangerous" information, Martin did not want me to have one.

"Science is 'dangerous,' " said Eduardo from the Commission on Social Communication.

I did not agree with him. I do not believe science is dangerous at all and I think people should be informed. It is a right, of each individual. But anyway, I did what Mr. President wanted me to do. In reality I did have access to information which, in the wrong hands, could lead us to disaster.

On D day I interviewed Charles Powell. Although his dossier stated he was thirty-two, he looked much younger. He was blond, very good-looking, with an easy smile and anxious eyes. From the first moment I liked him and thought he could be an effective element in the National Planning. His training in anthropology and psychology at Yale University was complemented by his work with the United States Army. Basically he had worked with transcultural research on child rearing practices, one of the topics we were most interested in. Charles had worked in Chile and Indonesia, and spoke good Spanish with a slight Chilean accent. He was a pleasant and quiet person who left a good impression in me. His wife was from Chile. He proved to be a very "international" psychologist, although when I was at Harvard I had believed American psychologists to be quite provincial.

"Why are you interested in working in Panama?" I inquired, knowing this was a required question in any interview.

"I have a very good opinion of the social changes you are making here. You're realizing what behavioral scientists have preached from their universities, without anyone taking them seriously. I want to better understand what you are doing and to contribute something to such an important social experiment."

Although a bit stereotyped, the answer pleased me. My question was as conventional as his answer. I do not think I was becoming paranoic like Martin! After all, this "gringo" young man could be truly interested in our Walden Three. Maybe I could make him my much needed reliable assistant in order to free me from excess work.

"You know in Panama we're modifying society, based on the principles of the experimental analysis of behavior. We imported the leading operant psychologists of the world who stayed with us for two years, outlined the most important plans and trained people who are now in charge of the social reform. We consider this change an experiment, a social experiment, like the French, Mexican and even the Russian revolution."

I stopped to observe his expression. He watched attentively and smiled, nodding his head every once in a while. This Charles was a good specialist in social reinforcement!

"My question is the following" I continued. "Do you think it's possible too go beyond experimental analysis? To go further than Skinner? To make an experimental *synthesis* of behavior instead of analysis?"

His answer was as technical as my question. I think he was taken a bit by surprise, probably because we had not touched upon the subject of experimental synthesis of behavior in detail, although the synthesis was the logical step after analysis. His answer was clear and intelligent. He did not commit himself with definite opinions, but explained his reasoning in a logical and coordinated manner. He indicated that it was possible to broaden the limits of experimental analysis without reducing accuracy or falling into speculation. The final limitation is total control of the environment, on a national level, as we were doing.

"Very good. Let's forget about the subject. I'm grateful that you've come to see us. I want to conclude by commenting what we all know, that in the United States as well as in Bolivia or in South Africa, the day of socialized medicine, planned economy and truly rational family planning will come. Misery will be eliminated; an army won't be necessary; education will be gratifying, not punitive; the family will be radically modified by emphasizing the couple instead of ceremony or reproduction. We all know this day will come for each country of the world: the United States, Bolivia, South Africa, all of them. Social classes and misery will be wiped out. Many people believe that this day is still far off and that they won't live to see it. Well, my friend, what we tried to do was to transform these ideals into reality, here and now; instead of talking about things, we did them."

"Wonderful!"

"That's why no one likes us. That's why they expect our Walden to collapse tomorrow or the day after tomorrow. But we're not going to satisfy them!"

He laughed and said, "I believe you're not! If there's something I can contribute to this gigantic undertaking, please let me know."

CHAPTER 22
MERCEDES AND FELIPE

Charles immediately became my assistant and I assigned him a considerable amount of my work. Gradually I introduced him into the fine details of my activities and entrusted him with responsibilities. I informed him about the strengths and weaknesses of the new government, its successes and its failures. It was wonderful having a confidential assistant. Charles became my right-hand with whom I could share a big part of my life and work.

We gave him an office in the Presidential Palace and entrusted him with confidential information. Charles always measured up to our expectations. He never disappointed us. He always did all his work with a strong sense of responsibility and obligation, and with a complete commitment to our goal of creating, with the help of science, a utopian society here and now.

Charles's and his wife's house almost became my second home, or better yet, my third one, right after Mercedes' and Felipe's house. In the few free hours I had, I visited Charles and his wife, or Mercedes and her son.

"You're putting too much trust in Charles," Mercedes pointed out to me one day. "You've given him all the 'top-secret' and confidential information about the wheels of government without previously subjecting him to a satisfactory test. You've given him too much too quickly. My dear, you're too naive. A person can't trust people as you have. You distrust no one. You don't believe anyone will exploit you or take advantage of you. But you'll see what people are like. Dave, I think it's time you use your 'native shrewdness,' as they say in the Andean countries."

"Hey, lady, don't be so hard on Charles! What he does and says seems honest and sincere to me. If you could only see the dedication and seriousness he puts in his work! He's always on time, respects deadlines and dedicates all his initiative and intelligence to persuing our ideals for the social reform. I've got all the confidence in the world in Charles."

"I hope he doesn't disappoint you. One never knows. I understand that you need a good assistant to help carry on your work and this man appears to have won your affection quite easily. At least you have more free time now, which is good. It's nice for me too, you know."

Every once in a while Mercedes, her son and I went to the country to walk and breathe fresh air. There were no high mountains to climb as in my country. Sometimes on these trips I missed my country and its mountains. But no, *this* was really my country, where I had dedicated all my energy and free time since leaving Harvard. What had happened to my sister and aged father? I hadn't heard much from them since the beginning of the New Era.

Mercedes, Felipe and I had formed a small family. It was like having a home again, a refuge amid the ups and downs of life. "The family is not born, it is made," was one of Mercedes' favorite phrases. It has to be cultivated just like a friendship; it really has to be created. Blood ties are probably the least important element in a family. What is important is affection and sharing life. Definitely, the family is not born, it is made.

"Had I been God, I would have made man very different," I half-jokingly told Mercedes and Felipe one day. "Obviously, I would have also made the world less complicated than it is. Man would have been simpler and at the same time more autonomous, more independent from other human beings. The day will come when the old and forgotten theory of a 'collective mentality' is revived, in the same way as it's been revived in the case of ants and bees. Each individual is just a part of a whole, submerged in an invisible multitude—a kind of collective unconsciousness, in Jung's style. Maybe by making a society like ours we're contributing to the arrival of this great multitude, this network, this group mentality."

"Do you remember Pablo Neruda? Somewhere he wrote:

> With only one life
> I will not learn enough;
> With the light of other lives
> Other lives will live in my songs."

"You scientists are known to be serious and cold," young Felipe intervened. "They say you don't have feelings and are only interested in test tubes and computers. It's strange to me that Einstein was a great violinist and that almost all great scientists are deeply interested in music, literature and so on."

"No, my boy. We're only interested in computers and test tubes. The rest isn't worth anything."

We laughed much to Felipe's surprise, who still was trying to understand us. Maybe he also felt that if he were God he would have made us all a little bit less complicated.

"One of Machado's phrases synthesizes scientific principles and world transformations to improve man's life. What interests people today is changing the world, not understanding it. One doesn't know how they claim to change it without first understanding it. Anyway, this is what many people are doing. We for one, especially our President. Machado wrote:

> Do you say that nothing is created?
> It does not matter. With the mud

Of the earth, make a cup
for your brother to drink."

It was nice to be with Mercedes and Felipe. However, life went on just as agitated as ever. I did not know what to do with the newly acquired free time I had, and this made me anxious. In order to escape from this anxiety I looked for new work which left me no free time. I checked what our Research Institutes (Criminology, Prolongation of Life, Family and Sexuality, and others) were doing. I planned visits to each of them in order to report to Martin and the rest of the National Planning Members.

I wanted to read about utopian societies, something that had always fascinated me since the time I was a junior high school student. I read the utopian works by Plato, Bacon and Thomas More. I read *Looking Backward,* and *Brave New World* by Huxley, *1984* by Orsell and *Walden Two* by Skinner, this last one for the fourth or fifth time. In reality our society was quite different from the rest. It was not as similar to Walden Two as we would have liked to believe. Since we worked with more ample and more complex parameters, we had to confront social problems (for example, criminology, economics, the military and police forces) that had no relevance in Skinner's Walden. We were not better or worse than the others, simply different.

Curiously enough, most of the utopian works were written in English. Not one existed in Spanish or French. Probably English-speaking people are more idealistic than we are, and that is why they write about such strange phenomena as "ideal" societies. Ours was not very ideal, in fact it was quite real, "down to earth;" in this aspect it resembled Skinner's *Walden.*

Our collective farms were a source of major pride. They strongly resembled the kibbutz of Israel and Walden Two. I have never seen anything as close to an "ideal society" as a kibbutz.. The way it emphasizes brotherhood and work, its abolishment of money, its great mysticism and group spirit, seemed to me so close to what every utopian writer, from Plato to Skinner had looked for.

Our collective farms followed the model of the kibbutz with respect to planning, collective decision making and the integration of mental and physical work. It was pleasing to see our young people, men and women, get up in the morning under the tropical sun, go to the fields, sow, harvest and plow the earth with a smile and a song—usually political—while driving the machinery:

> United in the struggle
> They won't move us!
> United in the strike,
> They won't move us!
> No, they won't move us!

We were an agricultural country. Accelerated industrialization did not imply we deserted the fields but mechanized its labor. Many problems had been solved, but many others, for example price control on agricultural products, were still a source of worry for our experts in agrarian economy. But the fields were filled with happy and strong men and women who worked from dawn to dusk, went home and washed, ate, read books, went to the movies, concerts or simply stayed with the family. "Little Peter's hour" was initiated in the country, they also had substitute mothers, schools with top-notch modern technology, where personalized education and the Montessori methods were integrated. They had everything except environmental pollution, stress, insomnia and existential anguish.

Those who participated in our collective farms said that they were not "simple farmers." Although illiteracy had been eliminated it was a daily struggle not to return to their previous patterns; to read the newspaper and listen to the radio. They had advanced considerably in this sense. The integration of mental and physical work meant that dedicating oneself to just one of these activities (for example mental activity, in the case of the teachers), was looked upon with suspicion and had very little prestige. Their ideal was an integrated, mature, strong and healthy man, with muscles and brains, who participated in the collective farm decisions, loved his wife and children and, at the same time, was aware of the latest singers, published books and even (which was almost an impossible goal) of the latest ideas of Sartre or García Marquez.

"We the people of the Third World are very close to the land," Mercedes said to me while she wiped the perspiration from her forehead and drew a deep breath. "Land is very important, it's the original life source of plenitude and nourishment. It's not uncommon that deep down our people still believe in 'Mother Earth' and would like to find in God a mother instead of a father, and think that God is Earth. That's why urban modernization plans of luring the farmers to big cities and leaving the country deserted will never work out. Farmers painfully part from their plot of land, as in the time of violence in Colombia when the countryside was filled with corpses and the rivers stained with blood. Our farmers want to continue being farmers. They want to get up early and go to the fields, drive a tractor, fill their baskets with oranges, and return with a smile to reunite with their wives and children to share a good dinner. Then talk to the children, observe the progress of the little one that has just started to walk, and check the homework of the daughter who wants to go to the university and become a teacher. At heart we are a simple, good, an unpretentious people, people who love the land and want to live in peace."

We were all farmers at heart. We felt that the family was important and it had to be preserved. We believed religion was important but religion without myths or fantasies, without gods, pseudoexplanations of the world or polemics against science. We loved children and nature; we were concerned about ecology and did not clearly understand politics.

There was neither delinquency nor crime in the countryside. If someone needed something it was given to him instead of forcing him to assault someone in one of the city's dark alleys. One always thinks about the assaulted and not the assaultant. I would be afraid to hold someone up and ask for money. My voice would tremble, the gun would shake all over, and I would be more terrified than my victim. It must be difficult to commit a crime, for heaven's sake! In the countryside, obliviously there was no delinquency, nor did we have pollution, stress or insomnia.

In the city we had all this. The problem of delinquency was complex and multifaceted. We handled it with behavioral modification (what else?). There was a very serious institute that dealt with this problem.

CHAPTER 23
DELINQUENCY AND CRIMINALITY

The Institute of Criminology was one of our government's prides. During the four year existence of the New Erra we had promoted research in many areas of human knowledge, especially in the behavioral sciences. Criminology was one of the strong points of the new government and many interested people came to Panama to study our successes in this so important and complicated area of human behavior.

The respective commission had started to study the problem in its contemporary perspective. It had established data about different types of crimes and offences, taking into account the people against whom the crimes were committed, and stated what were the important underlying causes. It had found an interaction between psychological, social and economic factors hard to be given an interpretation. It had not found any evidence to support the theory that crime resulted from biological factors (chromosome alteration of the XYY type).

"Delinquency doesn't have a biological basis and in this area, as in many others, the genetic influences on behavior isn't very important. Crime is a social phenomenon not a biological one, which argues against simplistic theories," I explained to my assistant Charles one day as we were going to visit an important rehabilitation center that was based on behavioral principles.

"So there is no evidence to assert that a biological substratum exists in people with criminal tendencies?"

"I don't think so. Besides, I think the situation is quite clear. The only thing the XYY syndrome seems to produce is a higher degree of impulsiveness. That's why they've tried to relate it to delinquency. It's curious how people love genetic explanations, which in the long run really don't 'explain' anything. To talk of 'innate' delinquency is to shut the door to the possibility of a causal explanation and a rehabilitation process. I think only the supporters of fascism feel comfortable with biological explanations of the criminal personality."

"And works on aggression like the ones done by Lorenz?"

"They're no more than pseudoexplanations, Charles. To say that man is destructive, that he's genetically inclined to crush his own kind, produces many conceptual problems. Recent studies on the origin of man, carried out by a brilliant, young scientist named Richard Leakey, from Kenya, demonstrate that when our species first appeared, it was within a context of cooperation rather than competition. Man was altruistic and cooperative ever since his beginning. To say that we're aggressive and destructive, that this is our 'animal nature,' is adopting a fascist and simplistic position.

I prefer to believe that we're cooperative and strive for common well-being. It's strange to me why the theories of Lorenz have come so far and have been taken so seriously. If someone believes in behavioral modification, he can't believe in genetic influence on aggression or things like that."

Various members of the Commission on Delinquency and Criminology were waiting for us in the Rehabilitation House. This commission was headed by a woman with tremendous drive and capacity for work. She also had a great ability to make people angry. Without a doubt, the area of criminology was quite difficult and complex. Besides, we were breaking new ground and, in a certain way, we were trying new alternatives. We were improvising (what a bad word!), that is for sure.

Beatriz, who was in charge of the Commission on Delinquency and Criminology, was young, as were all of us. She was not more than thirty but was burdened with two divorces and three children. She was very attractive, intelligent, and had a way with words. She always spoke clearly and I liked her contributions in the National Planning meetings.

After the formal introductions, Beatriz stated that her commission's work had been very successful and that it was indeed novel work in that area.

"In drawing the baseline of criminology in the country we are always confronted with economic factors. People rob and kill for economic reasons. That seemed simple and clear. One alternative was to create unemployment insurance, food coupons and other benefits that exist in some industrialized countries. But after discovering that such methods don't reduce delinquency, we thought of something else. We don't need unemployment insurance in Walden Three because we find jobs for everyone capable of working. Unemployment and sub-employment were eliminated. Nevertheless, delinquency remained relatively unchanged. In fact, it seemed that economic problems were correlated with delinquency but weren't the direct cause; they're related to it but aren't the main cause. Strange, isn't it? Another alternative were the biological explanations of a genetic nature, which didn't convince us either. We were left with explanations of another type, especially self-control and impulsiveness, which in the end appeared to be really important. Delinquents aren't capable of self-control, are easily excited, give a disproportioned response to a small stimulus, and have problems controlling their impulsiveness."

"Obviously there are many types of delinquents," added another member of the commission who worked under Beatriz' direction. The behavioral structure is different for a swindler, a murderer and a child molester."

"Of course," continued Beatriz, "this is true. With delinquency, it's necessary to operate on each behavior, its origins and its maintenance. A man who forges signatures has different motivations and is affected by distinct reinforcement schedules from the man who kills his wife's lover in a moment of rage. Criminology must take all these variations into consideration. Curiously enough, the classic theory doesn't worry about such problems."

"Our reform system is open," I commented to Charles. "There are two alternatives in the classical patterns for delinquency reform, associated with Germany and Sweden. The German pattern is quite rigid and uses a lot of aversive stimulation; the Swedish pattern has 'open doors' and a more positive approach. We're following the Swedish pattern since we're a permissive not a repressive society.

"Yes," added Beatriz, "That's right. But in reality we have our own pattern. Really it's neither the open door pattern, nor the German one. We continually insist on the learning of skills and the restitution for the crime committed. Society's traditional attitude towards delinquency can be explained from two different concepts: vengeance and responsibility. Man is responsible for what he does and if he commits a crime, he must pay for it; and society wishes to get revenge on the one who broke its laws and committed a crime."

"We don't feel the need to get revenge on our delinquents. Nor do we believe much in individual responsibility."

"By desemphasizing the myth of freedom," argued the young director of the Commission on Delinquency and Criminology. "The concepts of responsibility and vengeancy have no validity. We've investigated the causes of delinquency and have found many types of delinquents. There are individual differences among them, but especially there are group differences, depending on the crime commited: swindles, murders, rapes, and so on. In many cases there's an economic substratum. By giving employment and economic well-being to everyone in the New Era, those factors have ceased to be important. Of course, we're left with the possibility that the infantile deprivation that these people experienced still influenced their lives."

"Will we ever have a society without delinquents and criminals?" Charles asked.

"Yes, probably, but it's certainly not going to happen soon. By controlling everything, absolutely everything, the probability of criminal behavior will be greatly reduced. When everyone has been born and raised within the New Era, maybe crime will be totally eliminated."

"In other words, when all of us are dead," I concluded.

We walked around the Rehabilitation House, (previously called the National Prison for Women) and visited various wards. Contemporary Rehabilitation Houses were small and located in the country. The failure of the traditional jail systems had many causes, which we were investigating without pretending to have answers for all the questions. We had found a common denominator in all delinquents: the inability to delay gratification which is associated with impulsiveness. For a normal person it is easy to wait an hour to eat, or refrain from telling the boss what he thinks of him. On the other hand, this is tremendously difficult for a blossoming delinquent: he impulsively manifests what he thinks without any control; instead of thinking about hitting his enemy, he just hits him; instead of thinking about shooting three times a person who offended him, he actually shoots him. We have studied at length this impulsiveness and inability to delay impulse gratification.

We were teaching delinuents to postpone impulse satisfaction. In many cases we had established rehabilitation systems based on the token economy. The token served as a bridge between behavior and its posterior gratification. Time was gradually increased, from seconds to minutes, minutes to hours, hours to days and finally from days to years. It was a long, difficult process. We could not demand very much from the delinquents. Slow, gradual steps had to be taken. Obviously, nothing was left to chance.

This was a Rehabilitation House for women. Beatriz and her collaborators had chosen to show us the most difficult ward of all where they had begun to establish a token economy. Specific goals were stated by the inmates in agreement with the investigators. For a certain amount of finished work (for example, spun thread, knitted sweaters, cleaned wards, cooperation with the other inmates, followed instructions) they earned a certain amount of tokens. Each behavior had its price, which varied depending on the difficulty involved. This included negative behavior whose frequency had to be reduced (for example, "inappropriate sexual behavior," like masturbation in public or touching the breast of another inmate), and positive behavior (cooperation, cleanliness, appropriate language) whose manifestation had to be increased. We insisted upon implementing behaviors which would be useful to the inmates once they left the prison. Some of the behavior was relevant only to life inside the Rehabilitation House but presented special problems outside.

"After having modified the behavior of the women from the most problematic ward, they became assistants to modify behavior of inmates from other wards. They had learned well the principles of reinforcement schedules, response cost, and how to apply the token economy. They were good assistants, but the other inmates resented their privileged position of power. This was a bit difficult to handle. There were strike threats in the prison, and it would have been terrible if they had occurred. The women didn't want other inmates giving them behavioral norms, applying reinforcements, controlling the store where tokens were exchanged for objects or privileges. But by using more diplomacy and common sense and less science, we finally succeeded."

"Everything seems to be going quite smoothly."

"Yes. We have less than 200 inmates in a very big space. Each one has an individual room. They can bring along their small children who receive the care they need and, at the same time, remain with their mothers. Marital visits are allowed, which is very unusual since it has almost never been done in a woman's prison. Practically all the modern male prisons of the world allow marital visits but almost no female prisons do it. In this macho society it's tacitly accepted that men have sexual needs but women don't."

I though about Beatriz, her two husbands, three children and youthful charm, apparently 'hunting' for a man... instead of thinking of the inmates and their sexual life...

Everyone worked a lot. The women were always busy. There were classes on different subjects and many hours dedicated to resocialization. Each inmate received the money she earned for her work, after *paying* for her room and board. The women were not treated as "objects;" on the contrary, they were considered human beings with a past, future and a reality. Everyone knew each other, and knew very well why each one was in jail, but their crimes were not reinforced. There was no admiration for the one who had committed a worst crime than the others.

The principle of *restitution* was an important innovation in our penal system. Each delinquent had to make amends for the crime she had committed. The restitution was made to the afflicted person—or to his or her family—as well as to society, rather than spending idle years in prison. In murder cases it was impossible to restore life to the victim of a delinquent's impulsive deed; but the delinquent had to keep in contact with the victim's family, to see the magnitude of the real damage done and try to make restitution for the loss caused.

"Traditional rehabilitation has failed," said Beatriz's assistant, who was with us. "Classical humanism wasn't very effective. Nowadays we rehabilitate delinquents, considering how important it is to change behavior and attitudes, the whole person in relationship to his environment. We have to teach him how to *live again*. Just as education emphasizes intellectual, emotional, social ability and other factors, so does delinquent rehabilitation. We believe many analogies exist between the socialization (or humanization) processes of the new educational system and the delinquency rehabilitation processes. But since we aren't dealing with children, resocialization is much more difficult. It's necessary to unlearn a whole life's patterns of hate, unadapted behaviors, aggression, resentment, misery, pain and poverty—a lifetime of giving and receiving insults. We don't feel pity for delinquents. It wouldn't be congruent with the principles of the New Era. But we have *respect* and affection for them. We treat them as human beings and this has given very positive results."

"Rehabilitation implies a change in life style," said Beatriz to Charles. "We don't believe in a 'criminal mind' or in genetic factors to explain delinquency. We believe in open behavior. We also believe that the delinquent isn't a child and shouldn't be treated like one. We eliminate the prejudices and stereotypes of traditional criminology and practically start from zero: analyzing punishable behavior within its common environment, describing cases before explaining them, looking for the common denominator in various types of delinquents. We've found that the criminal and the person who punishes him are caught in a never-ending vicious circle of looking for vengeance; each one is taking revenge on the other. That's why we can see a high rate of recurrence among delinquents which alarms all criminology experts. We study the previous history of each delinquent. We're interested in his infancy and his history of reinforcement and punishment. We almost always find an unhappy childhood, with a mother who mistreated him and a father who excessively punished him and showed him a cruel and unjust world, and the need to act that way in order to survive. They were rules of a game the child couldn't understand. To revenge himself on the world, he committed his first crime and was sent to a juvenile home. He came seeking revenge for the bad treatment he had experienced there, and found himself once again in another jail. He went from one jail to another, each time committing more serious crimes, learning how to escape from justice, to express his anger and unhappiness, to avenge himself on the world from the injustices perpetrated against him. It's a vicious circle, the eternal search for vengeance. And traditional 'law and order' is doing its part to perpetuate this vicious circle."

"What alternatives do you suggest?"

"Rehabilitation and resocialization systems like this one, emphasizing reward rather than punishment; learning behaviors that will be useful outside prison. From here, inmates go to a Transition House where they can have an almost normal life. They're given a decent job and are freed—if we consider they've been rehabilitated—from the stigma of having been in prison. They're given a clean record and can begin anew. We have seen few relapses and up to now we're very happy with the results obtained."

"The length of time of imprisonment varies depending on the rapidity of the resocialization process and the restitution the delinquent must pay to the victim or his family. As Beatriz explained, they go to a Transition House. From there they take a stable, well-paid job without anyone knowing they were delinquents. There is, of course, follow up, but definite results are still to be seen, since its a new system . . . like everything else we're doing in this country during the New Era."

"This vengeance against the world is a curious factor in delinquency. It's associated with unjust and excessive punishment during infancy. Skinner already mentioned in his books the effects of punishment on neurosis; excessive punishment produces emotional and behavioral maladjustments, but I don't think anywhere he said it produces delinquency."

"No," I noted, "he didn't say so. And there was no delinquency or crime in Walden Two. Since it was a small society, economic, ideological, political, religious, ecological or criminal problems weren't taken into consideration. In Walden Three we consider these factors to be important. It's much easier to build a Walden Two than a Walden Three. In trying to apply operant principles on a national level it's necessary to consider many other parameters. Our society is more complex, with many variables that aren't relevant in Skinner's utopia."

"But we're closer to reality," Beatriz pointed out, "closer to the real world and its big problems."

CHAPTER 24
ECOLOGY

"Man is part of nature, just like amoebas, birds and stars," I commented to Mercedes days later.

The visit to the Rehabilitation House had pleased me very much and I think Charles was also greatly impressed. Now it was necessary to analyze the work of the Commission on Ecology which had to evaluate itself and begin to put the reforms from this evaluation into effect.

"Many times we forget about our biological nature. That's why we don't respect the limits of our organism; we pollute the air, destroy unrestorable natural resources and, finally, throw our ecological world off balance."

The great National Planning Hall slowly filled with people. The meeting included representatives of all the commissions since ecological problems are tremendously important. They were a kind of boundary for our civilization, a limit to the human capacity to scatter themselves throughout the planet, destroying forests and changing land into desert. The day of "silent spring" had already come to many regions of the world. Birds no longer sing in the morning because we had destroyed them with chemical products to poison insects which, at the same time, killed the birds. No link of the great ecological chain could be broken without affecting the rest. Each eco-system had to be respected, the elements we had destroyed had to be replaced.

The lecturer spoke profoundly and seriously, demonstrating the growth curves of the earth's population and the diminishing curves of natural resources. Being optimistic, the earth could produce oil for only twenty years more. Other mineral products were also coming to an end. Changes in the earth's ozone layer could cause unforeseen damage to human and animal life. There was a demographic explosion. Man consumed too many natural resources, uncontrollably polluted the air, destroyed ecological chains and created chaos in the biological balance that had existed in the earth for millions of years. The situation seemed really desperate. The biggest ecological catastrophe in the planet's history was about to occur. The two world wars were nothing and the black plague of the Middle Ages seemed no more than shadows by comparison.

Our goal of a society that would consume few natural resources, respect the planet's ecological balance and as far as possible avoid environmental pollution, seemed difficult to achieve. When a region of the world is developing industrially, it provokes a series of ecological damage. If Brazil builds a highway through the Amazon jungle, it gravely unbalances ecology. But it is done in order to develop a nation, to utilize its natural wealth, to feed its people.

"The dilemma that the industrialized world presents to us of the so-called 'developing world,' said our lecturer, "is very clear. They polluted the air, destroyed ecological balance to develop their industry and to become economic powers. But they demand that we, the poor Third World countries, don't do the same, that we respect the world's natural balance, that we don't cut down the Amazon jungle or exterminate wild animals of the forests. In this way the ecological balance of the planet will be maintained, but we won't develop ourselves economically. Those people of the "First World," the industrialized world, have already done it but they ask us not to, and they expect us to consider the problems of ecological balance and destruction of natural resources."

"This is true and important," Mercedes commented to me in a whisper. "In order to develop ourselves we must build factories, open roads and destroy forests. The industrialized world has done it, and now with the excuse of conserving ecological balance which still exists in our world, they demand us not to do so."

"Great dilemma."

"We will have to present a plan of economic development," continued the lecturer, "that respects biological balance, the ecosystems and prevents environmental pollution. We can't follow the example of the 'First World' and their society of consumption and waste. A man from a developed country consumes an average of ten times more resources than a man from an underdeveloped country. By demanding our place in an economically struggling world, we're competing for the few natural resources still left on this planet. We'll need more oil, more electricity and more atomic energy. This means we will enter into the price struggle, into the inflationary pyramid of the contemporary world. Once the whole planet is industrialized, once there are no forests or regions left to the exploited, the planet will resemble a desert and it will be almost the last day in time for our species."

The solution the Commission on Ecology offered was very complicated and implied a better understanding of natural systems, of organisms in relationship to their physical and biological environment. It called for a planned economy on a national level—which we already had—with ample and decided international collaboration—which we definitely did *not* have—and it seemed we were far from achieving. National Planning should go hand in hand with international planning, with a better worldwide economic order. Each region should produce whatever it is best able to produce. Agriculturally deficient zones could be dedicated to industry. But fertile land had to be used rationally for food production. Since it was impossible for all countries to adequably produce everything in an optimum cost-profit proportion, economic planning had to transcend national borders.

"Rational birth control is basic to the development of economic planning and an ecological perspective. In this aspect we've advanced considerably. The problem of overpopulation that so burdens the Third World with numerous prejudices and misconceptions, political and religious myths, has ceased to be a problem for us. This success has really allowed us to view the future with optimism. It's impossible for a couple to have all the children they're biologically able to procreate. By breaking the 'natural law' of infant mortality, which has been with us throughout history, we also broke the ecological balance of our species. Of course, we won't go back to the traditional solution of infant mortality; we're going to rationally plan the family. This should be done not only on a national level, but also on a worldwide level. Like the Chinese Republic, Canada, Germany, and other countries, we've made considerable advances in birth control. But the problem has to be faced on a world level, as well as a national one, and much less on an individual one.

"Another basic element in our ecological planning is the restoration of lost balance. We must plant new forests, clean the rivers, replenish the lakes with fish. Factories must be moved outside the cities. The Quality Environment Board plays an important role in this respect and is one of the fundamental elements of the Commission on Ecology.

"Technical development for recycling products holds a place of similar importance. Let's take for example the case of paper. Used paper can be recycled to produce new paper. If there were no more forests we'd realize the importance of these processes and stop wasting used products. Several metals can be recycled. Sewer water can be purified to be used again.

"Which takes us to the next point: garbage. Around each big city of the world exists and enormous belt of garbage that grows and grows. Everywhere the garbage problem is proving very serious and no one knows what to do about it. Before, people threw garbage into lakes, rivers and seas. As a consequence, the waters became sewers, and plant and animal life was destroyed. Currently, garbage is buried. Much of it needs thousands, even hundreds of thousands of years to decompose, since we haven't worried about producing biodegradable elements. The day will come when we won't know where to dispose of garbage. This isn't a problem of tomorrow, but of today. We need to increase the studies related to better garbage utilization and to produce only materials that are recyclable or degradable within relatively short periods of time."

The lecturer spoke of synthetic foods, solar energy and sea products for human consumption. He talked about reeducation programs for adults and early education with respect to nature for children. But in spite of everything, of population control, of restitution of ecological balance, of products' recycling, of garbage utilization, of synthetic meat, of solar energy and of exploitation of the seas, the situation appeared to be serious. We all left the great National Planning Hall worried and pessimistic.

In this small tropical country, what could we do to stop ecological destruction of the planet?

"If man would consider the coming generations, I think he would consume less and destroy fewer natural resources," Mercedes told me. "We're all selfish, worried only about our own well-being. We're not interested in what kind of world we'll leave for our children and grandchildren."

"The predictions are quite pessimistic, my dear. It appears that if the world keeps going like it is, we'll have children but not grandchildren. Our children's generation will be the last page in history."

CHAPTER 25
FREEDOM AND DETERMINISM

Obviously, what had to be changed was people's life-style, the society of consumption and waste, and the selfishness of man who thinks the world begins and ends with him. Let the other generations survive however they can! After all, maybe they will find a new source of energy, or perhaps the "Martians" will come and solve all of our problems.

By leaving nothing to chance in Walden Three, we could not depend on such far-fetched solutions to obtain sources of energy actually unknown to present-day man. Nor could we depend on the technical help of other planetary systems. Obviously, these things could occur and the future of our species was full of surprises. But since "futurology" is neither a valid nor reliable science, we could not rely on it. We had to find our own realistic solutions, here and now. It was difficult to stop the destruction of natural resources and environmental pollution. Since our country was just one among many, the solution had to be international and not limited within our national boundaries. We had to see what the great powers thought about ecological problems.

Our stubborn investigations, which always gave pessimistic results and alarmed First World governments, had an inevitably clear conclusion: the answer consisted in changing man's behavior, modifying society's consumption and waste. The solution relied not only on economic planning, but also on behavioral change. Governments knew this. Principal industrial countries frequently published reports on ecological problems. Everyone was aware that herein lay the solution. But no one did anything about it because they believed in Human Freedom (in capital letters) where each person was considered free to do as he liked: destroy forests, seas, throw garbage and waste around big cities, juggle oil prices and, as a consequence, ruin poorer countries unable to produce oil.

Obviously, no one could limit Human Freedom (in capitals). Supposedly only the communists committed such an unpardonable sin.

"In present day society there are few problems that are handled worse than the ones of freedom and determinism," I commented to Mercedes, Martin and Charles one afternoon in my office. "As a foundation of 'democracy,' freedom becomes a very serious thing, a kind of 'sacred cow,' and only behaviorism has been daring enough to question it and demonstrate that it's no more than a myth. Freedom and determinism are problems of words, not of facts."

"Since man is part of nature, his behavior is subject to laws; this is clear and obvious. There are physical, biological, psychological and social laws. Man isn't free to have a stomach ache or not to have it, to fly out of the window, or to grow five meters tall. It's schizophrenic to think this way. Man isn't free to decide whether to eat or sleep," added Mercedes.

"This physical, biological, psychological and social determinism is something that bores people a great deal," Martin pointed out. "Look at all the attacks that are published against us in the whole world. The strong powers watch what is happening in Walden Three with worried eyes, not because we make secret weapons, but because we have built a planned society and we believe in planning rather than freedom."

"But in schools the children are quite free," Charles dared to observe. "This has really surprised me. Children, the elderly and young people seem free and happy."

"Obviously, young man," I replied. "They're free and very happy. But they follow rules; order, logic and consequences are maintained. Even learning through discovery is subject to laws. Our children are 'free' and happy, it can't be denied. Being controlled doesn't mean we resort to chains, physical punishment, or bells for dinner and bedtime. This country has no curfew hour. Anyone can talk and write about what he wishes. But ours is a controlled society. In essence, the problem of freedom is a problem of words. We're always controlled in some way, even the people who talk most in favor of freedom and against control. The only thing we've done is explain the control contingencies and move them from man's interior to his exterior."

"The problem of freedom must be considered from a quantitative point of view," Mercedes noted. "It's not a matter of everything or nothing. I'm free to sit down or not, to eat fish today and meat tomorrow. Nevertheless, I'm not free to sit down for years or to eat only one product. Freedom is a matter of degree. In a reduced perspective, we all enjoy a certain level of freedom; we can choose among hundreds, one food to eat or a book to read. In a wider perspective, however, we have very little freedom. Certain foods please us, others make us sick. Certain books please us due to our history of previous reinforcement. Due to my own background, I like to read books on certain topics, like science, literature, biographies, travels, and pornography. I don't like them all. I'm relatively free to read about travel instead of literature, but I'm not absolutely free to read any books on any occasion."

"This is a matter of reinforcement contingencies, of behavioral consequences; and obviously of our previous behavioral history."

"It was Engels who stated that 'freedom is not to become independent from natural laws, but to know them and to make them perform in a planned way for specific means.' He insisted that this applied to external natural laws as well as to man's laws. According to Engels, 'these two laws can be separated only in the mind, but not in reality.' It's as if Skinner were talking, isn't it?"

I thought that by knowing our limits we could plan the New Era with more realism and a better probability of success. Control and planning make us internationately unpopular. We had to clarify doubts, specify why we considered freedom a pseudo-problem and concentrated our efforts on more important problems.

"Like the one of human brotherhood," I said out loud, although the previous ideas I had thought but had not expressed them openly. "Today people aren't very interested in the physical universe, but in the social one. People don't feel anguish because the world is expanding or because there exist 'black holes' that astronomy can't explain. On the other hand, they worry about the human and social world, about friction among groups, ideological problems, aggression and altruism. In one word: about man. Even religion has stopped verbal cabals about the existence of God as a 'motionless motor' and the basis of the 'perfection' perceived in the physical universe. It has begun to concern itself with the well-being of people, with misery, political and economic barriers that stand between them and a better life. Our century is one of man and his society. The last century was one of physical science. This one is the century of human science."

"We're no longer interested in understanding the world," Martin added. "Now we want to change it."

"To change man's world; to change family, infancy, education, individual and group behavior. Actually that's what we want to do. Our ignorance still remains, there are really enormous gaps in our knowledge. We don't even know how we perceive the world. We don't know what are the results of the interaction between the observer and the object observed. If we had another psychological structure, our world would be very different. We don't grasp the universe 'as it is,' but a small part of it through our senses or measurement instruments, and through the few concepts our intelligence can understand. It's a very reduced and limited world. But we've decided that it isn't important to understand the world, rather to *change it.*"

Basically this meant that we had stopped being scientists and were becoming politicians, political activists. We wanted to apply science, but for a practical end, not for a scientific one. This was an ideological and political aim.

"In other words," I said to Mercedes a couple of hour later when we were walking to her house, "the rules of the game have changed. A practical and social Walden Three should be able to compete with the big powers, each one having its own ideology and values."

"I never believed that the aim of Walden Three was scientific, Dave. I always thought it was practical. That's why Mr. President insisted so much on the improvisation matter. What we want to do is to better man's life; therefore we're more humanists than scientists."

"I think it has to do with a very curious interaction of behavioral histories. Martin is a man with a great need for power, with messianic fantasies of changing the world and finding his place in history. Thanks to one of those tours of life, he came to lead a country after a *coup d'etat*. For my part, I had the knowledge, but not the power. I felt lost in this country. My life lacked meaning and I felt empty: like water in a river, my life escaped through my hands. Martin sought my collaboration, accepted my suggestions. He dedicated all the nation's money of the construction of an ideal society. He was obviously the leader, the spokesman, the symbol of the New Era. It was *his creation,* his most important achievement. Faced by an undertaking of this magnitude, no one was going to remember its author as an alcoholic, a military man who took power by force. He was becoming a great statesman, a great social philosopher and even a great scientist."

"And you?"

"I had found a new dimension to my life, dear. I felt less lost in this country, which isn't mine anyway. As the president's scientific assistant, the brain behind the organization, I felt useful, I even think I felt less lonely and lost in the world."

"Why, my dear?"

"Ever since I was a child I have felt that way. I considered myself a foreigner in my own country, a foreigner at Harvard, and a foreigner here in this country. I was thirsty to belong, to put down roots, not to feel lost, as if I had come from another planet."

"This interaction of behavioral histories would explain Walden Three. And we, the Group of Ten, and all the members of the National Planning Commissions, found this to be a tremendously important undertaking, an opportunity that had never before existed of creating, with the help of science, an ideal society just like Plato and all the Utopians, from Aldous Huxley to Skinner, had wanted.

"They've been almost five years of struggles and efforts. I have worked a great deal and lived in a state of great tension, going from agony to ecstacy. How good it is to live that way! There's no routine or monotony, but on the other hand there is no time to rest nor to look up from work. I guess thanks to work, I quit thinking how lonely I am, and that someday we're all going to die. When Gerard Nerval died, they found a poem in his overcoat, which said, among other things:

They say he was a loafer, Bohemian and illusory,
who left the ink drying on his desk;
he wanted to know everything and in the end nothing he knew.
And one winter night, tired of life
he forever parted from the rotten clay
and went out asking: What was I doing here?

"When I leave, Mercedes, I'm not going to ask 'what was I here for?' I'll know then. That's why I feel young and full of energy, ready to confront whatever happens."

CHAPTER 26
THE END

For many months I have been waiting silently here in this prison for the hour to come. I guess they will judge and convict me for helping to build the New Era. There is no way of denying my participation in such an important social experiment; nor am I interested in doing so. I am a political prisoner. It is good that they have allowed me to write in peace and tranquility. That is why I have been able to complete the description of our work, how we built a utopian society here in the tropics, among the palm trees, next to the Caribbean sea.

Why did we fail? I do not know. I think we undervalued the importance of the political factors, the chess game of international politics. It was not because we closed our eyes to the outside world or thought that Walden Three existed in a void. No. Actually we worried a great deal about what the world thought of our scientific utopia. The criticisms were strong; and to our surprise, negative evaluations abounded, and finally just when it was starting to exist, one of the big powers intervened and ended our Walden Three.

We were not even five years old. We did not exist long enough to be able to make an objective evaluation of our society. No one can really say that we failed, rather that we were not allowed to carry through our social experiment. An incomplete experiment never gives definitive results and is no more than a pilot study. I believe we were victorious. I hope history shows I am right.

Who invaded us? It is funny how Martin distrusted China, the USSR and the United States so much. We wanted to be independent and play our cards, without protection or help from any of the big powers. We wanted to live and work without Marx or Jesus, without Mao or Lenin. Eliminating the army was a very daring move that deserved worldwide praise, but it endangered us. We became the easy prey of the great powers. We were a defenseless nation that believed in the "moral equivalent of war" but did not believe in war. We had educated our children to love peace. We insisted there should be no more wars. Political colors, stylish ideologies, territorial struggles, were immature problems to us. We were far away from such limitations. We were a young country that looked securely toward the future and had stubbornly decided to make its own way.

Ours was a different road. We were neither communists nor capitalists. We had a centralized economy and placed great importance on the formation of a new man for a new society. In this aspect we resembled the socialists of all times. We thought it necessary to respect man as an individual, give him happiness and the right to develop as a human being. In this way we resembled democrats of yesterday and today (without a doubt, more the ones of yesterday than of today)!

In a wide sense, we believed in science, not only physical science but also the science that studies the behavior of man and his society. It was a science relevant to a definite historical moment and a specific culture. Our socialist humanism, or humanist socialism, had been an innovation, a kind of mediating force in the contemporary world.

But we were a small unimportant society. In the world we represented nothing more than a slightly romantic and Quixotic alternative, which was very typical of Spanish people and tropical countries. We had wanted to form a "perfect" society, turning our backs on the big powers. Just as Don Quixote had departed to his journey amid protests and complaints from the people around him, who represented prudence and common sense, so had we started the task of making a better world in our own way. Maybe we were a little crazy, like Dox Quixote. Anyhow, if I could do everything all over again, I would do it exactly in the same way.

I think months of solitude have made me hard and at the same time sensitive. I have hardly talked with anyone in all this time.

They still have not brought me to trial. I have been well treated. They have allowed me to write, given me acceptable food and a comfortable cell. Nevertheless, I cannot sleep at night thinking about what has happened to Martin, Mercedes, her son Felipe, and all my collaborators from National Planning.

Charles's conduct especially hurt me. I had complete confidence in him and made him my main collaborator. He was my right arm and had access to all important government documents. That was my mistake. I was too naive. I should have realized that one goes through life surrounded by enemies, critics and envious people who pretend to be ones friend but bide their time to destroy one, to tarnish one's name, to take one's job. Since it had never happened to me, and since I had never been betrayed by my collaborators or my friends, I thought it would never occur. But the day finally came when it occurred like this.

I will never be sure if Charles was a spy sent to our country to find out state secrets. Probably he was. Martin, who was a paranoic with messianic fantasies, had cautioned me against Charles. I liked Martin but I also liked Charles, so I could not doubt either one of them or make decisions that would hurt either of the conflicting sides.

One day when Charles had left his office in the Palace, I found copies of letters that had not been filed because he had left quickly to attend a meeting. Although Charles had several secretaries, some of his work he did himself, which seemed very strange to me. Without really wanting to, I read the letters, although I did not understand much. They were addressed to Washington but made no sense whatsoever. They could have been written in code, but at that moment, I was absolutely unsuspicious. The letters were so simple that it was unusual. A secretary could write and file them with no great mystery. They were not addressed to the Pentagon. Of course not! But to Washington, yes. The contents were so simple and silly that I was confused.

I left them where they were and closed my assistant's private office again. I did not tell him that I had entered while he was gone nor in any way did I change my attitude towards him.

The invasion came a few weeks later. It is still hard for me to believe it. I do not know from where, but planes and ships arrived and took the capital. It was easy to do since we were without an army, as defenseless as children. We had moral strength, rather than military forces. The invaders encouraged the people to revolt against the dictatorship of Martin L. King, but no one did. Our people had forgotten that they were technically living under a dictatorship. In fact, everyone did what he wanted and there was no army to back up the government or to quell subversive plans. No one revolted. Nobody supported the invaders. However, nobody resisted either.

Still today, months later, it is hard for me to understand how all this happened. There was a military invasion, they took the country and overthrew the military dictatorship of General M. L. King. He defended himself, fought alone, escaped and, I think, finally committed suicide. He jumped into the sea from the Bridge of the Americas. It was very dramatic and histrionic, very much like Martin. Although it is also possible that they "helped" him jump. They arrested me and put me in this cell, where I have been ever since. I have taken advantage of the time to write and I hope someone will read what I have written and show certain sympathy for our efforts to create a perfect society, here in the tropics, with help from behavioral science and with the collaboration of a few idealistic young people. This writing resembles an intimate diary, and maybe at heart it is.

My collaborators were allowed to leave the country. Most of them went to Mexico and Venezuela where they were offered immediate political asylum. I do not know what happened to Mercedes and her little son.

The invading country justified its action by saying that we were oppressing our people and terminating Human Freedom (in capitals); that we were conditioning children and controlling their minds; that we were a "communist" society, right in the tropics, very close to Cuba, in the middle of the American continent. This was unacceptable. The invasion was similar to the Bay of Pigs in Cuba. In neither case did the people revolt against the "dictatorship" to satisfy the invading country . . . in order to justify its invasion. But we did not have an army, we did not have a strong godfather. We were not under the Soviet or the Chinese orbit. That is why we failed. Anyone who decides to create another ideal society must consider the political difficulties that we faced. No country is alone in the world. It cannot stand against everyone or plan a society without recognizing the interests of the strong powers of the world.

Although after thinking it over, I feel it is quite improbable that another country will try again to build an ideal society. If they do, they will not be pacifists as we were or try to be pure and simple as we did. A pacifist society, lover of nature and respectful of ecological balance, is an easy prey for those who are not pacifists, nature lovers or respectful of ecology.

I get a bittersweet taste in my mouth when I think of all this. We had the opportunity to convert humanity's most valued dreams into reality. We ended with traditional illnesses of our species. We looked for what united us with other men, not what divided us. We gave everyone food, a roof, work, and the possibility to love in one's way. In return we asked only that they respect each other's rights and the rights of nature.

Where are Mercedes and Filipe? What will the invaders do with the country now? Probably it will go back to the traditional capitalistic system; return to misery and unemployment and competition among men, hate and envy. Children will die again from controllable illnesses. Their parents will be unable to pay exhorbitant prices for medical services and medicines. As before, the calender will come with the traditional months. No one will have time to ponder or evaluate his life and work at the end of each year. Everyone will be busy buying and selling, consuming and destroying, polluting the environment and exterminating nature.

Why did we fail? I hope someday history will judge us fairly. Where could Mercedes and Felipe be?

> One sunny morning, spring sang
> but in seeing the house without you,
>   my whole body cried . . .
> You left me by the wayside, you
>   took my hope
> When the wheat was most golded in
>   the earth of my soul . . .
> You're my childhood song, the cry
>   of my guitar
> And upon the sea that keeps you
> I bring you French roses
> And the cry of my guitar . . .

"Professor González," said someone with a foreign accent knocking on my cell door.
"Yes, Sir. I'm ready. I'll be with you right away."